Teaching Students to Read Nonfiction

22 Easy-to-Use Lessons With Color Transparencies, High-Interest Passages, and Practice Pages—Everything You Need to Help Your Students Learn How to Read Textbooks and Other Nonfiction

by Alice Boynton and Wiley Blevins

SCHOLASTIC
PROFESSIONAL BOOKS

NEW YORK • TORONTO • LONDON • AUCKLAND • SYDNEY
MEXICO CITY • NEW DELHI • HONG KONG • BUENOS AIRES

Cover design by Josue Castilleja
Interior design by Sarah Morrow
Illustrations on pages 6, 12, 22, 26, 28, and 35 by Mike Moran

Copyright © 2003 by Alice Boynton and Wiley Blevins
All rights reserved. Published by Scholastic Inc.
Printed in the U.S.A.
ISBN 0-439-37652-1

7 8 9 10   40   09 08 07 06 05

Contents

Introduction

For many readers—including us—nonfiction is a gateway to new ideas and unfamiliar territory. We feel a bit like Dorothy in the *Wizard of Oz* leaving her ordinary black-and-white world and stepping into a technicolor world filled with fascination and wonder. Some consider fiction a magic carpet ride. But for us, nonfiction is the vehicle, and all the more exciting because what we're reading about is true; it really happened! It is hard for us to imagine not knowing about Cleopatra and her fate with the slithering asp, not learning about how Abraham Lincoln made our country a more civil and fair society, or not discovering the magic behind a slimy caterpillar turning into a delicate and beautiful butterfly.

Nonfiction has transported us to worlds old and new, filled our heads with information that has enriched our lives, and helped us survive in today's technologically-advanced world. Francis Bacon stated, "Knowledge is power." As teachers, we are constantly searching for ways to give our students the tools that will enable them to be successful. Teaching students to navigate, read, and comprehend nonfiction text not only gives them the information they need, it also gives them an avenue for exploring interests and satisfying their personal needs and desires. Knowledge *is* power! And we have the mandate to give that power to each and every one of our students.

Alice Boynton

Wiley B

Nonfiction Survival Guide

Nonfiction—What Is It?

This may seem like an easy question. But, what *really* is nonfiction? Nonfiction, also called *expository text*, provides information. Its purpose is to explain, inform, or persuade. You may be surprised by how much nonfiction surrounds us every day—newspapers, subway maps, instructions for changing a vacuum cleaner bag, recipes, and the dreaded VCR manual. Teaching students to read nonfiction, therefore, is essential as we teach them to develop as readers.

In grades 4 through 6, the emphasis in reading instruction changes from learning to read to reading to learn (Chall, 1983). As students progress through the grades, more and more of their reading is done in nonfiction, or expository, materials—content area textbooks, reference books, periodicals, and informative articles on the Internet, for example. The main purpose for reading these texts is to acquire information. Students need explicit instruction on how to approach these texts; it's a mistake to assume that since students can read a chapter book they can automatically read and understand a textbook.

Unlike narrative, which tells a story, expository text explains facts and concepts, many of them complex and difficult to understand. These texts use a whole different set of features and structures, which pose many challenges to intermediate-grade students if not explained and discussed. In addition, some students may still struggle with basic reading skills, making the challenge of nonfiction even more daunting. Ignoring the needs of students leaves them further behind; we need to offer them additional instruction and practice with reading skills and strategies.

Why Is It Challenging?

CONTENT

Reading and understanding expository text requires a high level of abstract thinking. Readers are called on not only to comprehend ideas that may be difficult, but also to extrapolate and remember the significant main ideas and to integrate them with other information from prior knowledge. Students must be able to recognize complex causes and effects, compare and contrast ideas, synthesize information from a variety of sources, and evaluate proposed solutions to problems as they read. This is tough work for developing readers!

VOCABULARY

Another major difference between narrative and expository text is the vocabulary that the reader encounters. Each content area has its own specialized terms that students do not come up against in stories—or in conversation either. Many of these terms are polysyllabic words that are more difficult to decode and pronounce. Here are some examples from typical science and social studies textbooks: *phytoplankton, photosynthesis, interrelationships, paleontologist, downtrodden, Parliament, Tlingit.* To compound the difficulty, many of the terms have unfamiliar meanings, such as the earth's *crust.*

TEXT FEATURES

Added to the demands of content and vocabulary are the special features of expository text—how expository text physically looks on the page. Unlike narrative text, which moves along from one chapter to the next without interruption other than an occasional chapter title or an illustration, expository text is frequently interrupted by headings and subheadings, pronunciations in parentheses, labels, footnotes, and a variety of graphics that must be carefully examined. Consider a typical nonfiction page (see example at right).

A student faced with a page of expository text may be so overwhelmed by the physical presentation of the material that he or she doesn't know where to begin!

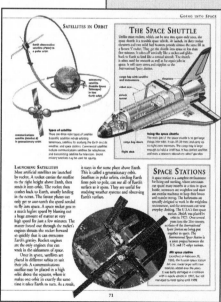

Typical nonfiction page

TEXT STRUCTURE

Another challenge to readers is the organizational structure of expository text. In contrast to narrative text, in which the plot flows from one event to the next, expository materials usually segment information into various topics.

The content is commonly structured in one of the following ways:

1. cause and effect,   4. sequence or time order,

2. compare and contrast,   5. listing or description, or

3. problem/solution,   6. a combination of the above.

In each new piece of expository text, the reader must uncover the organizational pattern in order to comprehend the relationship of ideas. Research has shown a strong link between a student's comprehension of expository text and his or her understanding of the way the text is organized (Seidenberg, 1989; Pearson and Fielding, 1991; Weaver and Kintsch, 1991).

Even if all these challenges make our heads swim, we must not forget the tremendous payoff that teaching our students to read nonfiction will have.

Why Is Nonfiction Important?

The ability to understand and write nonfiction is essential for school achievement (Seidenberg, 1989). Students will encounter a larger number of nonfiction texts as they progress through the grades, each posing special challenges. Students' success or failure in meeting these challenges has far-reaching consequences, as described below.

NONFICTION TEXT AND STANDARDIZED TESTS: THE CONNECTION

With the passage of the No Child Left Behind Act in 2002, students will be required to take high-stakes, end-of-year tests to determine whether or not they can be promoted. These tests ask students to read both fiction and nonfiction, compare the two texts, and respond to them in writing. Teaching students to navigate and comprehend nonfiction texts throughout the year will help them succeed on these critical tests. The ongoing teaching of useful strategies for comprehending nonfiction texts in both reading *and* content area lessons is far preferable to the sudden and intense test prep practice in the weeks leading to the test (an all too common practice in schools today). Students need time to practice and internalize these strategies. Frequent lessons and practice opportunities, such as those presented in this book, are ideal.

INCREASED WORLD KNOWLEDGE

Teaching students to navigate and read nonfiction texts gives them access to a large body of important and useful information—information that they are not exposed to in everyday conversations but need in order to succeed in school, develop lifelong learning habits, pursue their interests, gain necessary skills, and become well-informed and responsible citizens. Plus, learning about the world around us is fascinating!

Considerate Text:
This text is clearly written with signal words, the text features are appropriately placed, the text is logically organized and not visually overwhelming.

What Does "Reading to Learn" *Really* Mean?

The Stages of Reading Development
(based on Chall, 1983)

Stage 1: Grades 1 and 2

Initial Reading or Decoding: During this time, children develop an understanding of the alphabetic principle and begin to use their knowledge of sound-spelling relationships to decode words.

Stage 2: Grades 2 and 3

Confirmation, Fluency, and Ungluing from Print: Children further develop and solidify their decoding skills. They also develop additional strategies to decode words and make meaning from text. As this stage ends, children have developed fluency; that is, they can recognize many words quickly and accurately by sight and are skilled at sounding out the words they don't recognize by sight. They are also skilled at using context clues.

Stage 3: Grades 4 Through 8

Learning the New: During this stage, reading demands change. Children begin to use reading more as a way to obtain information and learn about the values, attitudes, and insights of others. Texts contain many words not already in a child's speaking and listening vocabularies. These texts, frequently drawn from a wide variety of genres, also extend beyond the background experiences of the children.

Stage 4: Throughout High School (Grades 9—12)

Multiple Viewpoints: During this stage, readers encounter more complex language and vocabulary as they read texts in more advanced content areas. Thus, the language and cognitive demands required increase. Students are also reading texts containing varying viewpoints and must analyze them critically.

Stage 5: Throughout College and Beyond

Construction and Reconstruction: This stage is characterized by a "world view." Readers use the information in books and articles as needed; that is, they know which books (and articles) will provide the information they need and can locate that information without having to read the entire book. At this stage, reading is considered constructive; that is, readers take in a wide range of information and construct their own understanding for their individual uses based on their analysis and synthesis of the information. Not all readers progress to this stage.

"The literacy demands required to thrive in society have changed significantly over the last several decades. These changes are particularly visible in the workplace" (Mikulecky in Lapp, Flood, and Farnan, 1996). According to the NAEP studies (1990), an increasing number of students graduate from high school lacking the basic literacy skills needed to succeed in today's job market. In 1990 the U.S. Department of Labor created the Secretary's Commission on Achieving Necessary Skills, also known as SCANS. This advisory committee was asked to identify the skills necessary for functioning in businesses today and offer suggestions for how schools can prepare students. The SCANS advisory committee suggests that teachers focus on the following five workplace competencies:

- Resources
- Interpersonal Skills
- Information
- Systems
- Technology

The commission does not recommend that schools prepare students for specific jobs, but rather engage students in long-term projects to develop these competencies. The strategies presented in *Teaching Students to Read Nonfiction* help students handle the literacy demands associated with each competency. Workers are required to communicate with each other and be proficient in the use of various forms of printed materials. Teachers can prepare students by teaching them how to navigate and comprehend a variety of nonfiction texts such as those listed on page 11.

How Can We Prepare Students

Research shows that understanding how text is organized helps readers construct meaning (Dickson, Simmons, and Kameenui 1998). It follows that students need explicit instruction in text presentation and text structure as an aid to comprehending expository text. If students learn to read the signposts that are guides to the organization of a particular piece of nonfiction, they will be better equipped to make their way through the material.

One approach to teaching students how to read nonfiction—such as content area textbooks—is to build students' skills in identifying and using the various characteristics found in this type of text. For example:

- Learning to **preview** the title, headings, and subheadings in a chapter of social studies text will enable the student to anticipate the main ideas that will be covered.
- Knowing how to use **text features**—graphic aids, such as diagrams, charts, graphs, and time lines—will allow the reader to

take additional meaning from them rather than viewing them as a disruption to the flow of the text. In addition, it will help students integrate this information with that provided by the text.

- Identifying the **text structure** will promote students' understanding and retention. Is the author comparing and contrasting life on the frontier with life in the cities? Is the text describing the physical characteristics of carnivorous dinosaurs?

Nonfiction surrounds us. The reasons for teaching our students efficient and effective strategies for tackling this type of text are compelling. What we must ask ourselves now is *How?*

Workplace Competencies	Nonfiction Text Demands
Using Resources: identify, organize, plan, and allocate resources, such as money, staff, and time.	A wide variety of material including:
Using Interpersonal Skills: work with others on teams, teach others, serve clients, exercise leadership, negotiate, and work with people of different backgrounds.	• newspapers • advertisements • manuals • instructions • forms
Using Information: acquire, organize, interpret, evaluate, and communicate information.	• announcements • graphs • tables • charts
Using Systems: understand complex interrelationships and distinguish trends, predict impacts, as well as monitor and correct performance.	• reports • pamphlets • e-mail and other forms of correspondence
Using Technology: work with a variety of technologies and choose appropriate tools for tasks.	

(Based on U.S. Department of Labor data, 1991)

How to Use This Book

—*Helen Rudin*

Teaching Students to Read Nonfiction provides 22 easy lessons that can be used during reading time or content area instructional time. The book includes:

- Easy-to-Use Text Feature Lessons
- Kid-Friendly Text Structure Lessons
- High-Interest Content Area Selections
- Assessment
- Purposeful Independent Practice
- Connections to Writing
- Tips for Choosing the Right Lesson

What's in a Lesson?

There are two types of lessons in this book: Text Feature lessons and Text Structure lessons. Text Feature lessons focus on the typographical and visual elements commonly found in nonfiction. Or, to put it another way, how the text looks on the page. Students are guided through the process of using these visual tools with a portion of text. For ease of use, we have provided the text on a color transparency for each Text Feature lesson. Students will encounter these same text features as part of a longer selection in the following lesson, which focuses on text structures. The lessons are organized so that each Text Feature lesson is followed by a Text Structure lesson that embeds the text feature of the previous lesson. The selections we have chosen are the type of nonfiction text that is typical of students' content area reading.

Text Structure lessons teach students how to identify the organization of a piece of writing. Repeated practice will help students internalize text structures so that they can use them more effectively to get information from their content area reading.

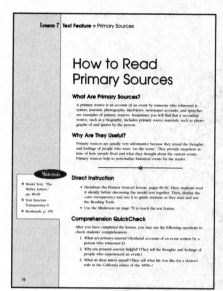

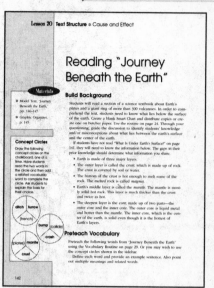

Text Feature lesson, see pages 78-79   *Text Structure lesson, see pages 142-144*

LEARNING ABOUT TEXT FEATURES

Let's take a closer look at the organization of a Text Feature lesson. It focuses students' attention on how to navigate the text and how to identify and use "tools," such as headings and boldfaced words, that serve as an aid to comprehension. In addition, many students need advance preparation in how to read and interpret the graphic aids they are most likely to meet in nonfiction text—maps, charts, graphs, diagrams, and time lines. Therefore, the lesson also includes one type of graphic aid and teaches students how to read and interpret it. The model text for each Text Feature lesson is included on a color transparency. Later, in subsequent lessons, the same feature will be embedded in authentic text just as students would encounter it in their science and social studies textbooks. At this stage, students will practice reading text, stopping to refer to a graphic, and then returning to the text.

Student Materials

For each Text Feature lesson, students will receive a step-by-step guide called **Reading Tools** on how to read the featured graphic aid. The accompanying **color transparency** of the graphic aid will facilitate group instruction and discussion.

The Reading Tools are summarized on a **Bookmark** for later reference. These are provided on pages 159-160. Students can cut out each bookmark and save it in an envelope labeled **Reading Tool Kit**. Students will find these brief "memory joggers" helpful when they come upon the same graphic aid in Text Structure lessons and in their content area reading.

The lessons covered in Teaching Students to Read Nonfiction *help students read:*

❋ *Diagrams*

❋ *Maps*

❋ *Charts*

❋ *Time Lines*

❋ *Primary Sources*

❋ *Graphs*

❋ *Social Studies Textbooks*

❋ *Science Textbooks*

❋ *Encyclopedia Articles*

❋ *Online Sources*

❋ *Text with Multiple Features*

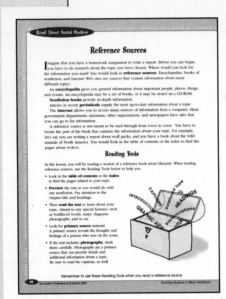

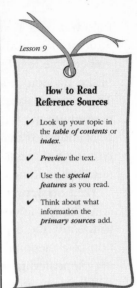

Reading Tools, Model Text, and Bookmark for a Text Feature lesson

LEARNING ABOUT TEXT STRUCTURE

Now let's focus on a Text Structure lesson. Informational texts have both a content and a structure. The structure is the organizational pattern *within* the text. It ties the ideas together. Understanding both the content and the structure is essential for comprehension. The first task is being able to identify the structure of a piece of text. The next task is knowing how to use that structure to organize the content (Just and Carpenter, 1987).

The 5 Most Common Structures of Nonfiction

Just like fiction, which has plot structure that students must learn and recognize, nonfiction follows basic structures, as well. Five kinds of text structures, or patterns of organization, are commonly found in informational texts:

1. **Description or listing** provides information, such as facts, characteristics, and attributes about a subject, event, person or concept. This organization is the most common pattern found in textbooks (Niles, 1965; Bartlett, 1978). Here is an example:

   The dinosaurs were four to eight feet long, about the size of kangaroos. They had small heads and long necks, and they walked on two or four legs.

2. **Sequence or time order** presents a series of events that take place in a time order. The author traces the sequence or the steps in the process. An example is:

Trouble had been brewing for more than 10 years. In 1763 Britain defeated France in the French and Indian War. Britain then tried to tighten control over its 13 American colonies and tax the colonies more heavily.

3. **Compare and contrast** points out the likenesses and/or differences between two or more subjects. For example:

The cheetah can run 70 mph. In the 1996 Olympic Games, Michael Johnson set a world record and captured the gold medal when he ran 200 meters in 19.32 seconds. That's 23 mph.

4. **Cause and effect** attempts to explain why something happens; how facts or events (causes) lead to other facts or events (effects). A single cause often has several effects. Also, a single event may have several causes. This paragraph describes causes and effects:

As the left plate slides down into the earth, it enters the hot mantle. Rocks in the sliding plate begin to melt, and they form magma.

5. **Problem and solution** describes a problem and presents one or more solutions to that problem. The following is an example:

Environmentalists are battling to save remaining native species. Scientists and private citizens are attempting to preserve 4,000 acres on the island of Hawaii by literally fencing them off against alien invader species.

Things would be nice and simple if every piece of expository text were neatly written in one clearly identifiable pattern. However, informational text is often complex, and an author may not use one text structure exclusively throughout a long piece of writing. It is more likely that only a section of text will be organized in a single pattern. For example, a chapter about weather in a science textbook may

- first discuss different kinds of weather conditions (*description/ listing*),
- then go on to explain the patterns that result in particular kinds of weather (*cause and effect*),
- follow up with a discussion of when a snowstorm officially becomes a blizzard or when a rainstorm is classified as a hurricane (*compare and contrast*), and finally
- close with what to do in the event of severe weather, such as a tornado (*problem and solution*).

The goal of text structure instruction is to enable students to recognize and use these structures flexibly so that they can make meaning from nonfiction texts.

Signal Words A good writer connects ideas within the text with words and phrases. These *connectives*, or *ties*, can act as signals to an informed reader who is trying to identify the text structure. The chart below shows some of the connectives that authors use to signal different text structures and the message they transmit to the reader.

Text Structures

Text Structure	Signal Words	Signal to Reader
Description or list	*to begin with, for example, for instance, most important, in front, beside, near*	A list or set of characteristics will follow.
Sequence or time order 1900 1950 2000 ①→②→③	*first, second, third, before, on (date), not long after, after that, next, at the same time, finally, then, following*	A sequence of events or steps in a process is being described.
Compare and contrast	*like, unlike, but, in contrast, on the other hand, however, both, also, too, as well as*	Likenesses and differences are being presented and/or discussed.
Cause and effect Problem and solution	*therefore, consequently, so, this led to, as a result, because, if ... then*	Evidence of cause(s) and effect(s) will be given or problems and solutions will be described.

This chart is Transparency 1

Text Structure Lessons

We can see why readers must be explicitly taught to recognize and use text structures. Text structures are critical for constructing meaning, yet they are often difficult to identify for the developing reader. Therefore, in the Text Structure lessons, two things happen:

1. **Students focus their attention on text structure.** They

are taught what the text structures are and what clues they can use to identify the organization of a particular piece of writing. Students will get multiple exposures to each of the text structures discussed above. And, of course, they'll have many additional opportunities to apply what they have learned in their classroom content area reading. The repetition will give students the multiple exposures they need in order to internalize the skill and become sufficiently proficient to use it independently.

2. **The selection provides students with another opportunity to practice and apply the skills** that were previously taught. The same features and graphic aids are embedded in informational text. A chart, for example, might be part of a science article just as students would encounter it in their content area reading. Students will practice integrating information from the chart with the information in the text.

USING HIGH-INTEREST CONTENT AREA SELECTIONS

As we have pointed out, the model texts provide students with an opportunity to apply their knowledge of text features to new texts. These pieces have been carefully selected to match grade-level science and social studies standards. For example, in social studies, fifth graders will be reading about United States history; sixth graders will explore the wonders of the ancient world.

Some of the topics covered in this book include:

Science: fossils and geology

Social Studies: U.S. geography, ancient civilizations and many more!

Assessment: Comprehension QuickCheck

Following the reading of each selection, the questions that are provided ask students to apply the skill in some or all of the following ways:

- identify the text feature and text structure
- explain the purposes of both
- use the text feature to get information
- generate other situations in which the text feature would be appropriate

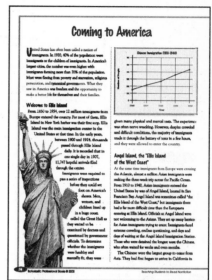

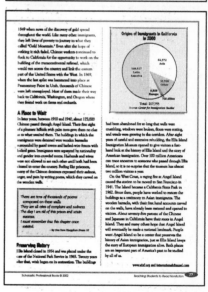

Model text for Text Structure lesson,
Lesson 6

APPLYING THROUGH PURPOSEFUL INDEPENDENT PRACTICE

A true measure of students' knowledge is their ability to use a particular skill on their own. Not only do we teach students to use text features, but we also provide opportunities for them both to practice getting information from these features in novel situations and to create graphic features of their own—such as charts, diagrams, and time lines—to organize information learned from a text.

A **reproducible** is provided for each Text Structure lesson. The reproducible can be used either in class, in learning centers, or for homework. The purpose of this reproducible is to check students' comprehension of the text they read, using a graphic organizer to record new learning. These graphic aids, such as main idea charts, summary charts, and Venn diagrams, are useful ways for students to organize the information in any text and serve as valuable models.

In addition, some of the **extension activities** at the bottom of the reproducibles ask students to organize new text using the text feature they learned about. For example, if students read about 19th century American life using a time line, they may be asked to read about a different time period in our country's history and create a time line to represent the major events. Repeated opportunities to read and create these text features will help students organize their thinking when reading and writing independently. And, these features can be applied to written reports and oral presentations!

CONNECTING TO WRITING

One of the ways to assess students' understanding of nonfiction text is by having them write **summaries**. Summarizing is an important reading strategy and critical writing skill. It involves selecting, organizing, and synthesizing the most important elements in a piece of text; and by using their own words, students demonstrate what they have learned. Summaries synthesize key ideas and details, are brief, do not contain the student's opinions, and are organized in a logical sequence. Summaries can be oral or written.

Summaries also require the reader to use all that he or she knows about the content of the text, as well as the text structure and its many features. Summaries are not easy for many students. Writing a good summary requires a great deal of modeling and guided practice (Hidi and Anderson, 1986).

In order to write a summary, a reader must be able to:

1. select the most important information in a text, thereby discarding the least important.

2. condense information by combining ideas or replacing a

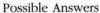

Possible Answers

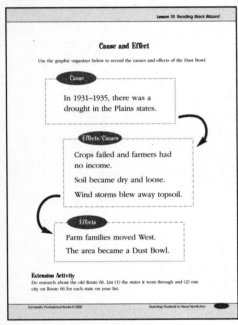

general term for a group of specific terms (i.e., "transportation" instead of "cars, trains, and planes").

3. record the most important ideas on paper in their own words.

Have students follow these steps to create a summary:

- Determine the main ideas, such as the main topic of the text. Use headings to help identify these main ideas.

- Look for information that is repeated. Be sure it is included only once. In addition, look for ideas that can be grouped.

- Look for the main idea sentence for each important section of text. It often appears in the heading or at the end of a paragraph.

- If you can't find a main idea sentence, think of one yourself.

- Write your summary. Be sure to use your own words and be brief (Cooper, 1993).

In addition, a great way to help students internalize important aspects of nonfiction is to have them apply these aspects to writing by **creating text using nonfiction structures and features**. For example, when teaching students how to read a text using sequence as its organizing structure, a great follow-up activity is to have them write a text using the same structure. (See chart below.) As students gain more experience using these text structures and features in their writing, they will begin to internalize them. Therefore, when they encounter these structures and features while reading, these texts will be easier to navigate and comprehend. The extension activities provide opportunities for students to apply their learning.

Remember—reading and writing are reciprocal!

Writing Assignment	Text Structure/Text Feature
Biography	Chronological order with time line
Report about a country or state	Description with map
Article for school newspaper about a school-related issue	Problem and solution
Report about a life cycle	Sequence with diagram
Essay about how something has changed over time, such as your town, clothing style	Compare and contrast
Speech about the effects of a new law or important news event	Cause and effect

Tips for Choosing the Right Lesson

How you use the lessons in this book will depend on your classroom set-up and your preferences. You may follow the sequence presented in the book or, since each lesson can stand alone, you may choose to dip in wherever you see fit. Here are several options that will work:

- **If your classroom is self-contained**, and you teach the content areas as well as reading and language arts, you may wish to approach each lesson as you would any reading skill—on a weekly or bi-weekly basis, following the sequence presented in this book. You can use the lessons to preteach text features and text structures, and later apply those skills to new text in social studies or science textbooks and periodicals. For example, you begin with Overview Lesson 1 on page 38 that introduces the text feature diagrams. At a later date, let's suppose your students are about to read a chapter about the water cycle in their science textbooks. You can first review the features of a diagram and then students can apply what they have learned to the new material in their textbooks.

- **As an alternative, you can teach the lessons in this book during your social studies or science block.** Preview the science or social studies textbook lesson for the week and identify the text features and structures your students will encounter. Then preteach those skills using the appropriate lessons in this book. For example, if the social studies chapter includes a two-tier time line showing the events in America and in Europe from 1770 to 1790, you can preteach with Lessons 17 and 18—the text feature lesson on time lines and the text structure lesson on sequence.

- **Another approach is to dip into just one part of a lesson.** You may use only a portion of the lesson based on student needs, reading levels, and time constraints.

IF . . .	THEN. . .
You teach in a self-contained classroom	Use the lessons in the sequence provided. You may want to revisit a particular lesson when students need to apply the skill to a new text.
You are a content area teacher	Use the lesson that is appropriate to the reading demands of the particular chapter you are using in your textbook.
You need more flexibility	Pick and choose portions of lessons to meet your current instructional needs.

Teaching the Lessons

Getting Started with Text Structure Lessons

Throughout our teaching careers we have encountered many students who have struggled with nonfiction text: *What do I look at first? How can I get through this? What does all this mean?* These questions no longer go unanswered. We now have powerful tools not only to help students navigate nonfiction text, but to get them on the right path to comprehension. Text Feature lessons focus on the graphic elements of nonfiction, and each lesson highlights one feature. Text Structure lessons require more preparation: building students' background knowledge and preteaching vocabulary. This section provides helpful strategies for these important aspects of Text Structure lessons.

BUILDING BACKGROUND

Let's stop for a moment to talk about how you can prepare students before they begin reading the content area selection.

Prior knowledge is the background knowledge of the subject matter that a reader brings to a text; in other words, what a person already knows about the topic based on that person's experiences and beliefs. Research (Cooper, 1993; Lapp, Flood, and Farnan, 1996) shows that activating prior knowledge before reading

- helps the teacher assess the accuracy of what students already know.

- helps the teacher identify gaps in students' prior knowledge—

information that students need to bring to the text in order to construct meaning.

- helps the learner construct meaning by making a connection between the new information and what is already known.
- helps the learner recall the new information after it is read.
- helps create motivation for learning.

Your role as teacher is to provide instructional scaffolds. Like the use of scaffolds in construction, you support, or lift up, students so that they can achieve what was not possible by themselves. As Vacca and Vacca (1999) state, "instructional scaffolding allows teachers to support readers' efforts to make sense of texts while showing them how to use strategies that will, over time, lead to independent reading." So, while you are not preteaching the information students will read, you are filling in instructional gaps or dealing with misconceptions that would otherwise impede learning as they read.

For example, when we were teaching a lesson on the role of Congress, the text contained the following opening paragraph (*Congress*, Patricia Ryon Quiri, Children's Press, 1998):

> *In 1776, the United States declared its independence from Britain. Americans wanted to have their own government. They were tired of Britain telling them what to do. They knew they would have to fight long and hard to become independent. The Declaration of Independence signaled the beginning of the American Revolutionary War.*

The rest of this excellent book details the Continental Congress, how the United States government was created, and how Congress works. But look at what you have to know to make sense of the opening paragraph. Our students needed to know:

- Britain is another name for England.
- In the 1700s, there was a group of people who came from Britain, or England, to settle this land.
- The land belonged to England. It was not called the United States at that time.
- The settlers did not make their own laws. They had to obey the laws of England.
- Being independent meant having their own country. Then they could have their own government and make their own laws.
- In order to achieve independence, the settlers went to war with England.

Without this information, our students would have had difficulty grasping the historical context in which the Constitutional Convention created Congress. For example, some of our students weren't aware that the United States wasn't even a country at that time. Many were unaware of our country's connection to England. These and other informational gaps were impeding their understanding of the book.

SMART CHARTS

How can a teacher bridge the gap between what students know and what they need to know? One recommended way is to use a Smart Chart (Scholastic RED, 2002). The difference between a Smart Chart and its classic cousin, the KWL chart, is the additional first column— Background. This column helps the teacher bring the students "up to speed" in terms of background information necessary to make meaning from the text. A Smart Chart:

- prompts students to think about what they already know.
- provides an efficient way for you to tell students important background information that they need to know.
- encourages students to organize what they know, what they want to know, and what they learned from a reading selection.
- helps students set a purpose for reading.
- provides a place for students to review and record what they learned.

Sample Smart Chart		**Selection:** The Louisiana Purchase	
B **B**ackground	**K** What We **K**now	**W** What We **W**ant to Know	**L** What We **L**earned
The western boundary of the U.S. in 1800 was the Mississippi River. U.S. hunters, trappers, and other pioneers were pushing westward into the wilderness past the Mississippi. Much of this land was owned by France and Spain. However, it was populated by many Indian Nations. France was engaged in a war with Great Britain and needed money to support the war effort.	In 1803 Louisiana was not yet a state. It was part of the Louisiana Territory, owned by France. Thomas Jefferson was president of the U.S. in 1803. The U.S. had fewer states in 1803 than it does today.	Why was it called the Louisiana Purchase? Who did we buy it from? How much did it cost? How big was the Louisiana Purchase?	Jefferson bought the Louisiana Territory from France in 1803 for $15 million. It doubled the size of the U.S. Lewis and Clark explored the territory for the U.S. government. Sacajawea, their Shoshone guide, helped them navigate the land and waterways. France called this territory Louisiana after their king, Louis.

There are many other techniques you can use. You may also wish to share information before reading in the following ways:

- Show a picture that illustrates the concept or time period, or sets the scene.
- Read a section from a book that explains the necessary prior knowledge.
- List key facts on the chalkboard and discuss them with students.

When students use prereading tools (such as a Smart Chart), prior knowledge is activated, helping them create a framework on which to hang new knowledge (Graves, Juel, and Graves, 1998).

To use a Smart Chart, follow the four steps as modeled in this classroom snapshot below.

Setting: Mrs. G. teaches fifth grade. Her class is reading a selection about the Louisiana Purchase. She displays the chart and says: "Today we are going to read a selection called 'The Country Doubles Its Size.' This selection is about Thomas Jefferson's purchase of the Louisiana Territory in 1803."

1. Look for ways to build on and connect to student ideas when they share what they know. This is an ideal time to dispel misconceptions and correct inaccuracies. Student prior knowledge goes in the "What We Know" section. This is Column head "**K**."

   Damien: I know that Thomas Jefferson was a president.
   Teacher: *That's right. He was the third president of the United States.*
   Emily: I know that Louisiana is a state.
   Teacher: *Excellent. But, in 1803 Louisiana wasn't a state yet. The United States only went as far west as the Mississippi River. Maybe we'll read why it was called the Louisiana Territory.*

2. Based on the gaps in students' prior knowledge, explain what they need to know so they can build "mental models," or pictures in their heads. This information goes in the background section. This is Column head "**B**." You will fill this out with students as you present the information that they have not already shared but need to know.

   [Teacher and students fill this out before reading.]

3. Use the "What We Want to Know" column to help students set a purpose for reading and to build their curiosity. This is Column head "**W**."

   Emily: Why was it called the Louisiana Purchase?
   Miguel: Who did we buy it from?
   Damien: And how much did it cost?
   Midori: How big was the Louisiana Purchase?

4. Use the "What We Learned" column to review important concepts in the text. This is Column head "**L**."

> *[Teacher and students fill this out after reading as a summary of their learning. Students explain how and where they got the information.]*

—*Lewis and Faye Copeland*

Remember, the goal is to provide a support for students on which to hang the information they will read. You are not summarizing, preteaching, or outlining what they will read prior to reading. If the information is not in the text, but necessary to understand the text, it needs to be pretaught.

PRETEACHING VOCABULARY

As you know from your own classroom experience, one of the many challenges facing students in their content area reading is vocabulary. Given the level of difficulty and the number of unfamiliar words that students are likely to encounter in a single chapter, you'll need to make several choices. One will be which words to teach. Another will be how to teach them. Research shows that the direct teaching of vocabulary can help improve comprehension when we follow these guidelines (Cooper, 1993):

- **A few critical words are taught.** Limit the number of words to 5 or 6 and be sure that they are key to the main ideas in the text.
- **The words are taught in a meaningful context.** The context should reflect the particular meaning of the word in the text.
- **Students relate the new words to their background knowledge.** Students are more likely to remember words linked to other concepts and words they already know.
- **Students are exposed to the words multiple times.** Students do not master new words after one presentation. Words have to be used in a variety of situations, including speaking and writing, before students "own" them.

Selecting "Just Right" Words

There are a number of considerations you will want to take into account when deciding which words to teach directly (Cooper, 1993).

1. Begin by reviewing the text to identify the main ideas. The key concepts will serve as your basis for determining which words will require direct instruction and also as a guideline

for activating prior knowledge.

2. Generate a list of words that are critical to understanding the main ideas that you've identified. These will be referred to as the "key-concept words."

3. Examine the text to see which key-concept words are defined or if their meanings are easily determined from context. Writers of expository text know that many of the words will be unfamiliar to students, so they include definitions within the text itself or context clues to help the reader determine the word's meaning. This is known as "considerate text." If the text contains such clues to a word's meaning, eliminate that word from your list because you will want to teach students to use these "unlocking the meaning" strategies during the reading of the text.

You'll want to keep track of these words on another list or highlight them on your copy of the text so you can take advantage of the "teachable moment" when students are reading. Students need these skills if they are to become independent at figuring out the meaning of unfamiliar words. Below are three types of context clues:

Types of Context Clues

Direct Definition: Direct definitions or explanations are the most obvious type of context clue. Words such as *is* and *means* signal that a definition or explanation of an unfamiliar word will follow.

*To many proud descendants of the Incas, the statue is a painful reminder of the destruction of the once-mighty empire of their **ancestors**. An ancestor <u>is</u> a family member who lived long ago.*

Restatement: Restatements are a type of context clue that uses different words to say the same thing. A restatement is often signaled by *or, that is,* and *in other words,* and is usually set off by commas.

*Jefferson asked Meriwether Lewis to lead an **expedition**, **or** exploring party, into the Louisiana Territory.*

Compare/Contrast: Comparisons or contrasts are a kind of context clue that likens or contrasts an unfamiliar word or concept. Words and phrases, such as *like, just as, similar, different, in contrast,* and *on the other hand,* signal that a comparison or contrast of an unfamiliar word will follow.

***Unlike** the **indigenous** people of North America, the new settlers from England were unaccustomed to using the plants that grew along the East Coast.*

4. Some of the words on your list may contain structural elements that students can use to determine meaning. These words will not need to be taught directly. If they are stumbling blocks during reading, encourage students to use what they know about prefixes, suffixes, and root or base words to unlock meaning.

> ecology: *ology* = the study of
> geology: *ology* = the study of
> bicameral: *bi* = two
> biped: *bi* = two
> hydroelectric: *hydro* = water
> dehydrate: *hydro* = water

5. Decide which words will probably be familiar to your students. These words may require only a quick review and not intensive instruction.

6. The words that remain on your list will require direct instruction. But if there are still too many, use your judgment to pare the list down to 5 or 6 words. You will not want to overwhelm students, so your final choice should be no more than 5 or 6 words.

Teaching the Words

It is critical that students "own" the words we teach them. That is, students should be able to use the new words in speaking and writing. There are four levels of word knowledge (Dale and O'Rourke, 1971):

Level 1: "I never saw it before."
Level 2: "I've heard of it, but I don't know what it means."
Level 3: "I recognize it in context—it has something to do with…"
Level 4: "I know it."

The goal of word learning is Level 4.

VOCABULARY INSTRUCTIONAL ROUTINE

Here's an effective routine we have used with our students to introduce and teach new vocabulary (Carnine et al, 1997).

Vocabulary Routine

Routine	Lesson Model
1. Use a visual, such as a picture/ photo in the text to be read.	**Teacher:** This is a statue of a pharaoh.
2. Model the pronunciation of the word.	Teacher writes the word **pharaoh** on the chalkboard. **Teacher:** *This word is **FAIR-oh**. You say it.*
3. Provide a synonym or a definition for each word. One way to define a word is to tell its class and then specify characteristics that make the word different from others in the same class.	**Teacher:** *A **pharaoh** was a king in ancient Egypt. The rulers of other countries had different titles. In England, the title is king or queen. In China and Japan, the ruler was called an emperor or empress. A ruler in India was called a rajah.*
4. Check students' understanding.	**Teacher:** *What is a pharaoh?* **Student:** A pharaoh was what a king was called in ancient Egypt.
5. Give examples and non-examples. Students tell whether or not the example illustrates the definition of the word and explain why or why not.	**Teacher:** *Was King Tut a pharaoh?* **Student:** Yes, he was a king of ancient Egypt. **Teacher:** *What about King George II? Was he a pharaoh?* **Student:** No. **Teacher:** *Why not?* **Student:** Because he was king of England. **Teacher:** *Does Egypt still have a pharaoh?* **Student:** No, not any more. It has a president.
6. Provide vocabulary activities so that students may review the words and their definitions.	Activities may include cloze sentences, matching words and definitions, and writing sentences that use the vocabulary words.

Work With Words To review the words on subsequent days, place them in a larger context by connecting them to other words and concepts students know. This will deepen their understanding. Here are some effective strategies.

Vocabulary Teaching Strategies

Strategy	Purpose	When to Use	Comments
Concept or definition (word web)	Help students become independent word learners by teaching elements of a good definition	• Expository texts	Good support of strategy for independently inferring word meanings
Semantic mapping (web map)	Integrate prior knowledge and vocabulary learning	• Before or after reading • All texts	Develops in-depth word knowledge
Semantic feature analysis	Develop word knowledge by comparing words	• Before or after reading • Expository text and some narratives	Often more effective after reading
Hierarchical and linear arrays	Develop word relationships	• After reading • All texts	Encourages students to compare and contrast words
Preview in context	Use text context to develop word meanings	• Before reading • All texts	Must have text with good context clues
Contextual redefinition	Use context to determine word meaning	• Before reading • All texts	Useful when texts do not provide strong context clues
Vocabulary self-collection	Help students learn self-selected words	• After reading • All texts	Makes students responsible for vocabulary learning

(Cooper, 1993)

Vocabulary Graphic Aids

Word Web

Word Map

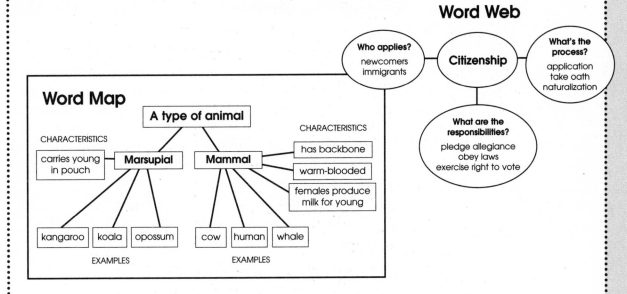

Semantic Feature Analysis

	Polar bears	Tiny shrubs, Short grasses	Deciduous trees	Tall and short grasses	Cacti	Vultures	Canopy of large leaves	Algae
Aquatic Biome	+	+	−	−	−	−	−	+
Desert	−	−	−	−	+	+	−	−
Temperate Forest	−	−	+	+	−	+	−	−
Tropical Rain Forest	−	−	−	−	−	+	+	−
Tundra	+	+	−	−	−	−	−	−

Linear Array

Hierarchical Array

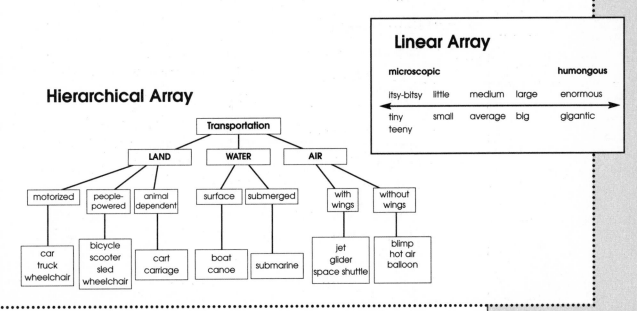

Provide Practice With Vocabulary Words

The goal of all vocabulary instruction is to get students to be able to use the words in speaking and writing. Two useful activities include the following.

Oral Practice Read aloud sentences such as the ones below. Have students listen for and identify the error in the sentence. It may be an incorrect pronunciation of the vocabulary word or an incorrect word. Compare the vocabulary word and the error. Ask students how the words are different: *What sound is different in each word?* Write the two words on the chalkboard and have students point out the spelling differences. Have students repeat the sentence using the correct word. For example:

1. We saw the adult butterfly emerge from its chrystalis. (*chrysalis*)

2. An antphibian can live equally well on land or in water. (*amphibian*)

3. Carnivals are animals that eat meat. (*carnivores*)

This practice improves students' auditory sensitivity and acuity in addition to reinforcing the vocabulary word.

Written Practice Students can write cloze sentences for the vocabulary words. (Some students may find it easier to write a sentence that includes the targeted word and then rewrite the sentence using a blank for the word.) Have student partners exchange papers and complete the sentences.

1. A _____ is a cocoon. (*chrysalis*)

2. A turtle is an _____ because it lives on both land and in the water. (*amphibian*)

3. Herbivores eat only plants, whereas _____ eat meat. (*carnivores*)

Assess Vocabulary Words

Have students react to open-ended statements about each vocabulary word. Their answers and explanations will allow you to assess their understanding of the word quickly (Beck, 1985). Write a *Yes* or *No?* statement on the board. Ask students to respond *yes* or *no* and give a short oral explanation for their answers. Explain that there is no right or wrong answer. Students will be giving their opinions. See the following for how this strategy might work in the classroom.

Yes or No?

1. Carnivores are dangerous to people. ___ yes ___ no

2. A chrysalis is an amazing "shelter." ___ yes ___ no

3. An amphibian is like a fish. ___ yes ___ no

Tips for Writing Yes or No Statements

Writing good yes or no statements for this portion of the assessment can be tricky. When writing a yes or no statement, ask yourself, "Can the statement be answered by both 'yes' and 'no'?" If so, you've written a good statement.

Statements that lead to clear answers are of little value. For example, most students would answer "yes" to the statement, "Carnivores like to eat meat," unless they didn't understand the term *carnivore*. However, the statement, "Carnivores are dangerous to people" can be answered in many ways. Some students may say "yes" and point to meat-eating animals that have attacked people in the past. Other students may say "no" and point to meat-eating animals that are friendly to humans.

Therefore, the student's answer is not as important as how the student justifies the answer. This justification and the subsequent discussion are what reveal a student's knowledge of a word and, therefore, are the true benefit of the exercise.

Here is an example of teacher-student dialogue.

Teacher: *Read the first statement. What do you think—yes or no?*

Student 1: I say no.

Teacher: *Why?*

Student 1: Because carnivores eat things like leaves, not people.

Teacher: (Notes that student does not know the meaning of carnivore. Turns to the next student.) *Paul? Do you agree?*

Student 2: I said no, but for a different reason. Even though carnivores are meat-eaters, most wouldn't harm people unless they were in the wild and felt threatened or were very hungry.

After reading this section, you should now be able to answer the following questions:

✓ How do I build a student's background knowledge?

✓ Why is it important to do this?

✓ What graphic organizer can aid in building background and monitoring learning?

✓ How can I preteach vocabulary words?

✓ Which words should I preteach?

✓ How can I use a small set of key words to build general word knowledge?

✓ What can I do while students read to continue building vocabulary skills?

Word-Learning Tasks

As you preview a selection, you may be trying to identify only those words that are totally unfamiliar to students. However, there are actually four different relationships between words and concepts that may be barriers to reading comprehension (Alverman and Phelps, 1998; Lapp, Flood, Farnan, 1996). These four relationships are called **word-learning tasks**.

1. The first task is **learning to read known words**. We may associate this skill exclusively with beginning readers, but less able readers in the intermediate grades may still be learning to read words that are in their oral vocabularies. For example, students may know the word "weather" when they hear it, but errors in decoding may result in (weet HER), which of course renders it meaningless.

2. The second task is **learning new meanings for known words**. Most students will be able to read the word "front," but will they all know what it means in relation to weather? There are a great many familiar words that have other precise meanings in particular content areas, and students will be frustrated by them: "*What does a* crust *have to do with the earth? We're not talking about bread!*"

3. The third word-learning task is **learning a new word for a known concept**. A student may not know the word *hereditary*, but he probably has the concept that he gets his curly hair from his grandmother and his brown eyes from his father.

4. The fourth and most demanding task is **learning a new word for a new concept**. A student may not know that bats use *echolocation* to find bugs and other edible treats. With this process for locating distant or unseen objects, sound waves are reflected back to the surface (i.e., the bat).

SUMMARY

The "Prepare to Read" portion of each lesson should take approximately 20 minutes. It is essential that key terms be defined and students' background knowledge activated before they begin the task of navigating a new piece of text.

So, you and your students are now ready to tackle nonfiction texts. In the following section, we provide two detailed, sample lessons carefully spread out over two weeks of instruction. These overview lessons are designed to help you introduce students to nonfiction text, and nonfiction text features and structures. They will also assist you as you establish classroom procedures for teaching nonfiction texts throughout the year.

Easy-to-Use Nonfiction Lessons

−*Milton Berle*

Overview Lessons

How to Read Nonfiction How many of you have ever taught a child to ride a bike? You may recall the eagerness of the child to just hop on and go, the frustration after the first few unsuccessful attempts, and finally the jubilation when the child realizes he *can* do it. Learning any new skill requires good instruction, lots of practice, and often a fair amount of time. When we teach our students a new skill, we give them opportunities to test out their use of the skill, a safe environment in which to make mistakes if they're not quite there, feedback and encouragement to help them correct their mistakes, and then time to revel in their learning when they know they have mastered the skill.

Two Weeks, 30 Minutes a Day When it comes to learning about non-fiction, not only do our students need multiple teaching and practice opportunities, but they also need to get started on the right foot in order to understand what text structures and features are and why they're important. To help your class get started in the best possible way, we have provided two detailed Overview Lessons; each overview lesson first introduces a text feature and then a text structure. We have carefully selected two pieces of nonfiction text that our students have enjoyed. Then, in just two weeks, 30 minutes a day, we will help you establish the routines and procedures you can follow all year to succeed in teaching your students how to navigate nonfiction text and learn from it. Here's a glimpse of what you'll do:

Overview Lesson 1: "Return of the Wolves"

DAY 1: INTRODUCE NONFICTION TEXT

You'll introduce your students to nonfiction text and find out what they know about this important text type. Engaging your students in a conversation about great nonfiction books they've read, topics they're interested in reading about, and nonfiction books you like and recommend, is a great way to motivate students and set up a classroom environment in which nonfiction is read, discussed, learned from, and enjoyed.

DAY 2: PREPARE TO READ

You'll introduce your students to a nonfiction article called "Return of the Wolves." As you display the article on the transparencies, you will build background and preteach vocabulary using the teaching routines provided (see pages 29–31). Since these steps will be used all year, it's beneficial to take the time to discuss in depth each aspect of each routine to help you and your students become familiar with the routine. You will also teach students how to preview text in order to navigate the text and its features effectively.

DAY 3: TEACH TEXT FEATURES

You'll read the nonfiction article, "Return of the Wolves," focusing on one important text feature, reading a graphic aid—a diagram, in this case. As you teach students how to use the graphic aid to obtain information, you will reinforce the Reading Tools that students should learn for navigating nonfiction text.

DAY 4: TEACH TEXT STRUCTURE

You'll revisit the text to focus on its text structure—compare and contrast. Since learning and identifying text structure is more difficult, it is best to address text structure *after* students have had the opportunity to read and work through any comprehension difficulties in the text. This second reading will allow students to focus on more sophisticated aspects of the text since comprehension difficulties will have been addressed in the first reading.

DAY 5: CHECK COMPREHENSION AND APPLY TO WRITING

After two readings of the text, you will now take the opportunity to formally check students' comprehension *and* their ability to apply their learning to new texts. As the year progresses, students will become more adept at identifying and learning from text structures and features. Remind students that this is hard work, takes time, and is worth the effort. Soon, reading nonfiction texts will not only be easier, but it will be fun as well!

Overview Lesson 2: "Hanging By a Thread"

DAY 1: REVIEW NONFICTION TEXT

You'll review the key characteristics of nonfiction text with students. You will discuss the text features and text structures that students have encountered in recent readings. You will also emphasize how knowing those features and structures will make nonfiction text easier for them to read and understand.

DAY 2: PREPARE TO READ

You'll introduce your students to a nonfiction article called "Hanging By a Thread." As you display the article on the transparencies, you will build background and preteach vocabulary using the teaching routines provided. You will also teach students how to preview text in order to navigate both text and text features effectively.

DAY 3: TEACH TEXT FEATURES

You'll read the nonfiction article, "Hanging By a Thread," focusing on one important text feature, reading a graphic aid—a chart, in this case. As you teach students how to use the graphic aid to obtain information, you will reinforce the Reading Tools that students should learn for navigating nonfiction text.

DAY 4: TEACH TEXT STRUCTURE

You'll revisit the text to focus on its text structure—problem and solution. This second reading will allow students to focus on more sophisticated aspects of the text since comprehension difficulties will have been addressed in the first reading.

DAY 5: CHECK COMPREHENSION AND APPLY TO WRITING

After two readings of the text, you will now take the opportunity to formally check students' comprehension *and* their ability to apply their learning to new texts.

These two weeks of lessons will help students understand what a text feature is and what text structure is. They will lay the foundation for future Text Feature and Text Structure lessons.

Week 1
"Return of the Wolves"

Day 1: Introduce Nonfiction Text

WHAT'S SPECIAL ABOUT NONFICTION?

Explain to students that they will be reading a great deal of nonfiction not only throughout this year, but also every year as they move up through the grades. Point out that students already read nonfiction because it surrounds us. Every time they pick up a newspaper to find out how their favorite team is doing, whenever they follow a recipe, or read a movie review, they are reading nonfiction.

Nonfiction gives information. It explains, informs, or persuades. Point out that nonfiction materials are quite different from a story or a novel and that reading nonfiction often presents more challenges than reading fiction. Make students aware of some of the reasons for this by discussing the following characteristics of nonfiction. Show examples from a chapter in your social studies or science textbook.

Materials

* Model Text, "Return of the Wolves," pp. 43–44

* Transparencies 2-3

* Graphic Organizer, p. 59

* Bookmark, p. 159

Characteristics of Nonfiction Text

1. Nonfiction looks different from fiction.
   - In addition to a chapter title, there are headings and possibly subheadings throughout the text.
   - There are often a variety of fonts and type sizes on each page.
   - Words in a paragraph may be boldfaced or italicized.
   - Diacritical markings may follow some words to show pronunciations.

2. Graphic aids are usually included. They explain the information in the text or give additional information and must be examined carefully with attention to captions and labels.

3. The topic being discussed probably contains unfamiliar vocabulary that is specific to a subject area and not likely to be heard in general conversation. There are often multisyllabic words, such as *photosynthesis*, that may be difficult to pronounce.

4. There is a great deal of information to be understood and remembered.

Tell students that the good news is they can learn how to navigate their way through the challenges of reading nonfiction. And although they may find it hard to believe, many of the features that make nonfiction seem daunting actually are "clues" to help them understand what they're reading. Reassure students that they can learn how to identify these "clues" and use them to read more skillfully. And it doesn't take a Sherlock Holmes!

Ask students to share experiences they've had with nonfiction. Questions such as these may get the ball rolling: *What nonfiction have you read in the last couple of months? Do you enjoy reading nonfiction? Why or why not? When you read an article or a biography, do you look at the illustrations and read the captions or do you skip them?*

Show students your copy of *Teaching Students to Read Nonfiction* and explain how it will help them (see Think Aloud).

Day 2: Prepare to Read

BUILD BACKGROUND WITH A SMART CHART

Students will read an article about an experimental program to increase the population of wolves; wolves were classified as an endangered species in 1973. In order to comprehend the article fully, students will need to understand the concept of an *ecosystem*.

Create a blank Smart Chart and distribute copies (see page 24) or create one on butcher paper.

- **What We Know** Ask students to tell what they know about wolf populations as they exist today. As students share information, record it in the second column, What We **K**now. Through your questioning, guide the discussion so that students discuss what they know about the habitat of wolves, how numerous or scarce wolves are today, what wolves need in order to survive, and who their enemies are. General facts about wolves, though certainly interesting, will not be helpful background for comprehending the article, so try to keep the focus of discussion on the article's main idea.

- **Background** In the first column of the chart, **B**ackground, record the background information that students need to understand the article but did not mention during their discussion.

  The gaps in your students' prior knowledge will determine what among the following information you should share with them before reading:

  - An ecosystem is a community or habitat of living and nonliving things. An ecosystem can be as small as a rotting log or a fish tank, or as large as a forest or an ocean.

  - In an ecosystem, living things such as plants and animals depend on each other and also on nonliving things such as air, water, and soil.

Think Aloud

Throughout the year, I'm going to teach you tools that you can use when you read nonfiction. These tools will make it easier for you to understand encyclopedia articles, periodicals, and your science and social studies textbooks. They'll probably help you do better on tests, too. Tomorrow we'll read an article about wolves and learn more about how to read nonfiction.

- A change in an ecosystem affects the plants and animals that are part of the system. For example, if there is not enough oxygen in the water of a fish tank, the fish will not be able to breathe and so will die. Without the fish to release carbon dioxide when they breathe, the plants will not be able to make food, and they will die.

- The needs of people sometimes conflict with the needs of an ecosystem. When making a decision that affects them both, each one's needs are taken into account.

- **What We Want to Know** Finally ask students if the discussion raised questions that they would like to find the answers to. List these under What We **W**ant to Know.

- **What We Learned** Complete the chart after students read the article.

PRETEACH VOCABULARY

Preteach the following words from "Return of the Wolves" using the Vocabulary Routine on page 29. Or you may wish to use the knowledge rating chart shown on page 41. After each student rates his or her knowledge of the words, follow up with a discussion of which words are the easiest, most difficult, most unfamiliar to the greatest number of students. Encourage students to share what they know about the words. The discussion will also give you an idea of how much knowledge students bring to the concepts they will be reading about.

Define each word and provide an example sentence. Also point out prefixes, suffixes, and related words.

- **activists:** people who take action in support of a cause. *Activists held a rally to raise money for Save the Whales.*

    The suffix *–ist* means "a person who does or is an expert in." Other common words with this suffix are: artist, pianist, scientist, journalist, typist, chemist.

- **livestock:** animals used on a farm or ranch or raised for sale. *Cattle, sheep, and pigs are livestock raised on ranches.*

- **ecosystem:** a habitat where living and nonliving things affect each other. *The ecosystem in a fish tank must be balanced in order for the fish to survive.*

    Eco is a Greek word part that means "environment" or "habitat." *Ecology* has the same prefix. Ecology studies the relationship between living things and their habitat.

- **prey:** (v.) to hunt other animals for food. *African lions prey on antelopes and zebras.*

    The word *prey* can also be a noun which means *an animal that is hunted by another animal for food.*

Knowledge Rating Chart

How Much Do You Know About These Words?

	Can define	Have seen/heard	Have never seen/heard
activists			
livestock			
ecosystem			
prey (*verb*)			

DISPLAY TRANSPARENCY

Display the **color transparencies** of "Return of the Wolves."
Distribute copies of the model text, "Return of the Wolves." Explain
that the **Reading Tools** section of each lesson deals with how nonfiction text looks on the page. Each tool highlights one of the features in
the text and explains how it helps the reader. Guide students through
the reading. Use the Think Aloud provided.

Preview Routine

An activity that will be extremely helpful to students before they
begin to read a selection is previewing the text. A preview informs
students about the content of the material and gives them a framework for reading. Use the following procedure to demonstrate the
usefulness of previewing the text:

- First, have students read the title of the selection. Ask them
  what the text will be about. Write the title on the chalkboard.

- Then, ask students to read heading "B" and discuss what it tells
  them about the content of that section. Record the heading.

- Ask students what they expect to learn from the selection.
  Record their answers.

- After students complete the reading, ask them to tell in two or
  three sentences what the text was about. Compare what they
  say to their original prediction.

- Point out that the chapter title and the headings were the main
  ideas of the text students were about to read. These features
  told students what to expect.

Think Aloud

*The title of the article tells
me that I'm going to read
about wolves going back to
a place where they had
once been.*

*As I preview the introduc-
tory copy and the headings,
I see that two of the main
ideas in the article are that
wolves are an endangered
species and that there is dis-
agreement about returning
them to the wild.*

*So I predict this article
will give the reasons why
some people think wolves
should be returned to the
wild and why other people
think they should not.*

*As I read the article, the
map will help me under-
stand where wolves are
found. The diagram will
explain how wolves fit into
the food chain. When I'm
finished reading, I'll understand what different groups
think about returning
wolves to the wild.*

Read About Science

Nonfiction Text

Nonfiction is a type of text that gives you information. A science article is one kind of nonfiction. It contains information and special vocabulary about a science topic. The first thing you may notice about a nonfiction article is that it looks very different from a page in a novel. You will probably see a title and several headings, all in different sizes. There may be photos with captions and special graphics such as a map, a diagram, a graph, or a chart. Sometimes nonfiction has several of these features all in the same article. There may be a lot going on.

All this "stuff" can seem very confusing! However, each one of the features on a page is there to help you better understand what you are reading. Think of them as tools. If you know how to use them, they'll work for you.

Reading Tools

- First look over the whole article. Think of it as a **preview** of what's ahead—like the preview of a movie.

- Read the **title**. It tells the topic of the article.

- Read the deck, or **introduction**, and the **headings** to find out the main ideas you're going to read about. They are clues that let you know what to expect.

- **Predict** what you're going to read about. Say to yourself, "This article will be about…"

- Notice the **special features**. Are there diagrams? Do you see a map or a chart? These graphic aids illustrate what you've read or add new information. Don't skip them!

- Now start to read the article. Look for helpful features in the text. Words in **boldfaced type** signal important vocabulary that you'll need to remember. **Pronunciations** let you know how to say difficult words.

- At some point, the author may ask you to look at a special feature, such as a chart or diagram. If this happens, stop reading and go to the **graphic aid**. Study it carefully and read any **captions**. Then go back to the text and continue reading from where you left off.

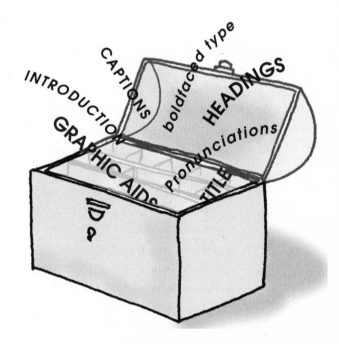

As you read "Return of the Wolves" remember to use the Reading Tools.

Return of the Wolves

Endangered wolves could make a comeback, but first, people have to agree that "the big bad wolf" is not so big and bad after all.

Once the howl of the wolf was heard all over the wilderness in the United States. But by 1900, only a few thousand wolves roamed free in the U.S., mostly in Minnesota and Alaska. In 1973, the government put wolves on the endangered species list.

Animal activists are working to bring back the wolf. However, some farmers and ranchers worry that this meat eater will endanger their way of life.

In an experimental program, 31 wild wolves were brought from Canada and released in Yellowstone National Park in the last two years. Nine wolf pups were born in the park. Now, animal activists want to repeat this success story in New York, Maine, New Mexico, and Arizona.

The Wolf Debate

In New York, dairy farmers worry that wolves will attack them or their **livestock**, but animal activists disagree. "The big bad wolf image is a lie," says one activist. "There is no record of wolves ever hurting humans."

On the other hand, wolves have been known to attack livestock when the wolves' normal food supply was scarce. A farmer near Adirondack (ad-uh-**RON**-dak) Park in New York, where wolves may be released, is worried. "Big dairy farms are 200 miles from the park. That's within the traveling distance of wolves," he said.

Similarly, in New Mexico, ranchers worry about wolf attacks on their cattle. In response, one group of activists, Defenders of Wildlife, has agreed to pay for livestock lost to wolves. They paid a

This gray wolf pup and its mother are two of about 200 gray wolves living in the Northwestern U.S.

from *Scholastic News*, V59, No. 17, February 21, 1997

rancher near Yellowstone National Park after a wolf killed two sheep. They also returned the wolf to Yellowstone.

The Balance of Nature

Animal activists point out that wolves are an important part of the **food chain** (see diagram, below). They hunt and eat large grazing animals. In the Adirondacks, deer and moose herds have grown so large that there is not enough food for them. Activists say wolves will prey on the sick weak animals. That will keep herds healthy and maintain the balance of the **ecosystem**.

It may be years before wolves are released in New York. However, wolves may be returned to New Mexico and Arizona far earlier. Animal activists hope wolves will become a familiar sight across the U.S. Until then, wolves will be common only in fairy tales.

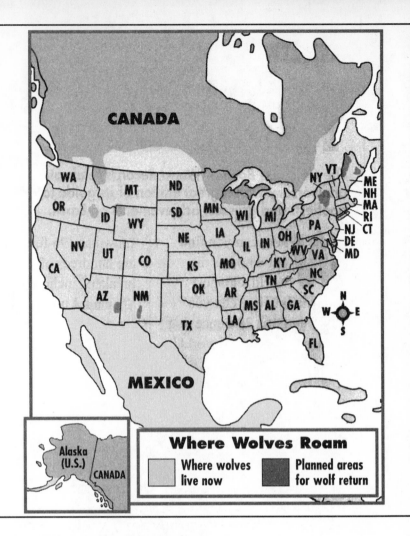

Where Wolves Roam

Where wolves live now

Planned areas for wolf return

How the Food Chain Balances Nature

Animals depend on plants and other animals for food. This feeding relationship is called a *food chain*. This diagram shows you how a food chain works.

1. Producers: Plants and other organisms that provide food for animals make up the first link in the food chain.

2. Herbivores: These are animals that eat only plants. Called "prey," they are hunted by meat eaters.

3. Carnivores: These meat eaters feed on herbivores. They are also called "predators." When they die, their remains fertilize the ground and help plants grow.

Day 3: Teach Text Features: Diagram

Put the transparency on the overhead and ask students to pull out their copies of the article and their Reading Tools. Then guide students through the lesson below.

READ THE SELECTION

- Have students read the article aloud, section by section. Guide students as they apply the Reading Tools they learned.

- When they come to the direction "See diagram, below," tell students to stop reading and go to the diagram.

- Use the Minilesson to teach students how to read and interpret the diagram. Be sure that students are able to find the place in the article where they left off in order to resume reading.

- After the Minilesson, have students resume reading the article.

Minilesson

Teaching the Text Feature
Graphic Aids: Diagram

Introduce: Discuss with students the expression "A picture is worth a thousand words." Explain to students that graphic aids, such as maps, charts, and diagrams, are pictures that present information. Sometimes a written explanation can be complicated and difficult to follow. A graphic aid can show the same information visually. It helps the reader visualize ideas so that he or she can better understand and remember them.

A **diagram** gives the reader a picture of how a process or a relationship works. Some diagrams illustrate information in the text. Others add important new information.

Explain how students should read a diagram:
- Read the **title** to find out the topic of the diagram.
- Read the **deck** to learn the main idea and other information about the topic.
- Read the **steps** in the correct order. Numbers guide them from one step to the next. Start at number 1.
- Read the **label** and explanation or caption.
- Then study the **illustration**.
- Go on to the **next number** and continue reading.

Model: Use the Think Aloud to model reading the diagram.

Guided Practice/Apply: Have students read the diagram. Then ask volunteers to retell the information in their own words.

Think Aloud

The title of the diagram tells me that I'm going to read about the food chain. The deck, or introduction, explains what the food chain is.

Starting at step 1, I read the label, "Producers," and the caption. The caption explains what's taking place in the diagram. Then I look at the picture that illustrates it. Next, I go on to step 2 and do the same thing. I follow the numbers to read the steps in the correct order.

When I'm finished, I understand how the food chain works. I also know why wolves are an essential part of the food chain and the balance of nature.

Day 4: Teach Text Structure

WHAT DO MY STUDENTS NEED TO KNOW ABOUT TEXT STRUCTURE?

Text structures are more difficult to identify and use than text features. Therefore, when introducing a new text structure it is best to work with a text students have already read. This familiarity with the content will enable students to focus on more sophisticated aspects of the text's organization. You may think you're being repetitive, but your students will need to hear again and again (1) what text structures are and (2) what clues students can use to identify the text structure of a piece of writing.

Students are most likely to meet five text structures in their textbooks and other nonfiction materials. Display **Transparency 1**, as you discuss each one.

- Problem and Solution
- Compare and Contrast
- Cause and Effect
- Sequence
- Description

Some texts are organized around just one of these structures. An article explaining what is being done to foster the return of the peregrine falcon to its habitat, for example, may be structured around problem/solution. Other texts may present information using two or more text structures. That same article about peregrine falcons might have opened with a passage about how the use of insecticides harmed the eggs of the birds—cause and effect—and then gone on to show what is being done to correct the situation— problem and solution.

WHAT'S ITS VALUE?

Students may wonder why it is important to identify text structure in nonfiction. They need to know that a reader who is aware of the pattern that is being used can anticipate the kind of information that will be presented. If we know that a text is organized around compare and contrast, we expect to read about the likenesses and differences between people or events. This gives us a framework for connecting the ideas and remembering them.

HOW CAN IT BE IDENTIFIED?

The text structure of the article "Return of the Wolves" is **compare and contrast**. In the opening passage, the author explains that the wolf, once prevalent in wilderness areas, is now on the government's endangered species list. Animal activists are trying to build up the wolf population by reintroducing wild wolves to certain areas.

In the next passage, the author informs the reader that there are different opinions about what the activists want to do. The article goes on to **compare and contrast** the viewpoint of the animal activists with that of opposing groups.

Authors often include words and phrases as signals for the reader. *However, on the other hand, but,* and *although* serve as clues that the text organization is compare and contrast.

Headings are also clues. The heading **The Wolf Debate** tells the reader that there are differing opinions about the proposed solution. It's important for students to become aware of possible clues in the text and to look for them as they read.

Have students reread "Return of the Wolves," this time focusing on the text structure that the author has used to present the information. Use the Minilesson to teach the concept of text structure.

Minilesson

Teaching the Text Structure: Compare and Contrast

Introduce: Explain to students that a writer of nonfiction organizes information in ways called text structures. The information that students read in their science and social studies textbooks and in magazine articles is most often structured in one of five ways. The writer may:

- **compare and contrast** information,
- present information in a **sequence** of steps,
- put forth a **problem** and offer **solutions**,
- provide a detailed **description**,
- explain the **cause and effect** of an event.

Discuss the importance of identifying how text is structured. It alerts you to how the text was written. This knowledge can help you organize your thinking as you read. For example, the reader thinks, "The writer is going to compare and contrast. That means I'll be reading about how things are the same and how they are different. I'll look for those likenesses and differences as I read."

Model: Use the Think Aloud to model how to determine text structure.

Guided Practice/Apply: Have students reread the article. Distribute copies of the graphic organizer for compare and contrast. Ask students to fill it out as they read. You may wish students to work individually or as a group.

Think Aloud

When I previewed the article "Return of the Wolves," I read in the deck that wolves are endangered, but they could make a comeback. Then I read the heading, "The Wolf Debate." I know that a debate is an argument. So I expect the author to compare and contrast different opinions about the wolves. I think that the organization of this article will be compare and contrast.

As I read, I found that I was right. Some of the clues I used were the words however, but, *and* on the other hand. *These words were signals that the author was comparing and contrasting different opinions.*

By the end of the article, I knew what the different opinions are about returning wolves to the wild.

Day 5: Check Comprehension and Apply to Writing

COMPREHENSION QUICKCHECK

After you have completed the lesson, you may use the following questions to check students' comprehension:

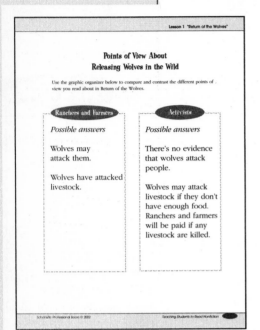

1. What clues helped you figure out the text structure? *(The deck was a clue that people did not agree about what could be done for endangered wolves. Also, the heading "The Wolf Debate" was a clue that the article was also going to compare and contrast different opinions about endangered wolves.)*

2. How did knowing the text structure help you? *(I was able to understand and remember why some people were in favor of releasing wolves in the wild, and others were against it.)*

3. What new information did the diagram add? *(The diagram showed how the food chain works, so you could understand the part wolves play in the ecosystem.)*

4. Why was the map included? *(It shows at a glance the areas where wolves are found now and where activists want to return them. You can also see that there are not many areas in the United States where wolves live, especially compared to Canada.)*

5. What side of the debate would you be on if you lived near a wilderness area? *(Answers will vary.)*

Independent Practice: Writing

Have students write a summary of the article. Ask them to include the following:

- what is being proposed to save endangered wolves,
- the point of view of each group involved in the debate.

Web Links

www.nwf.org	National Wildlife Federation
www.wcs.org	Wildlife Conservation Society
www.wolf.org	International Wolf Center

Points of View About
Releasing Wolves in the Wild

Use the graphic organizer below to compare and contrast the different points of view you read about in "Return of the Wolves."

Ranchers and Farmers

Activists

Week 2
"Hanging By a Thread"

Day 1: Review Nonfiction Text

Review with students the key characteristics of nonfiction text. Use **Transparencies 2 and 3** to review text structures and text features.

Day 2: Prepare to Read

BUILD BACKGROUND

Students will read an article about endangered plant and animal species in Hawaii. Use the Smart Chart routine (p. 24). The gaps in your students' prior knowledge will determine which of the following information you should share with them before reading:

- Plants and animals that are not native to a particular ecosystem may have a negative effect on the existing plants and animals. When new plants and animals are brought into a country from another land, they may injure or destroy local plants and animals.

- In Australia, for example, a man imported 24 wild rabbits from England in 1859. He released them on his property. Today there are over 200 million rabbits in Australia. They have damaged the Australian environment and are a major pest to farmers.

After students finish the article, it will be interesting to compare what has happened in Hawaii with the situation that was described in "Return of the Wolves." Instead of the ecosystem being affected by the loss of a particular species (wolves), the ecosystem in Hawaii has been affected by the addition of species that were brought to the islands from other lands.

PRETEACH VOCABULARY

Preteach the words below from "Hanging By a Thread" using the Vocabulary Routine on page 29. Or you may wish to use the graphic organizer shown in the sidebar. Students can add other examples that they know about or from their reading.

Define each word and provide an example sentence. Also point out prefixes, suffixes, and related words.

- **biologist:** one who studies living things and the way they live and grow. *The biologist studied the plants and animals of the rainforest.* The prefix *bio-* means "life," the suffix *–logy* means "the study

Materials

* Model Text, "Hanging By a Thread," pp. 55–56
* Graphic Organizer, p. 77

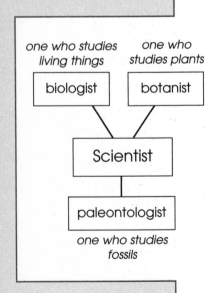

one who studies living things — biologist

one who studies plants — botanist

Scientist

paleontologist

one who studies fossils

of," and the suffix *–ist* means "one who does or is an expert in." A related word is *biology,* the study of living things. The prefix *bio-* is also found in the word *biography,* which is an account of someone's life. The suffix *–logy* is part of many words related to science. Some examples are *zoology,* the study of animals; *meteorology,* the study of the atmosphere, winds, and the weather; *archaeology,* the study of past times and cultures.

- **paleontologist:** one who studies fossils found in rocks. *The paleontologist found the fossil of a seashell at the foot of a mountain which was evidence that the land had been under water thousands of years ago. Paleontology* is the science that studies ancient forms of life as revealed by fossil remains in rock.

Day 3: Read the Selection

Distribute copies of "Hanging By a Thread" and display Transparencies 4 and 5. Guide students as they apply the strategies they have learned for navigating text. When students encounter graphic aids while reading, remind them to use the Reading Tools. In addition, a Minilesson on reading the chart is provided below.

Minilesson

Teaching the Text Feature: Chart

Introduce: Remind students that graphic aids, such as charts, organize information in a way that is clear and easy to understand. Discuss that the same information could be explained in written form, but it would take many sentences and even paragraphs to state it. Students should understand that they can get the data at a glance from a chart. And it will be already organized for them. Reading and understanding charts is a skill that students will find useful throughout their lives.

To read a chart, students should do the following:
- Start with the **title** to learn the topic of the chart.
- Then read the **column headings** and the **labels** for the rows. They let students know what information the chart shows.
- Next read the **caption**, if there is one. It adds information that readers may need to understand the chart.
- Now they are ready to access the information in the chart. Read across a row to find specific information for each column.
- Read down a column to find specific information for each row.
- Use the information to make comparisons and draw conclusions.

Model: Have students follow along on their charts as you use the Think Aloud in the sidebar to model how to read a chart.

(continued on next page)

Think Aloud

I see that this chart will give me information about endangered and threatened species in the United States and abroad. Each column contains different information. For example, the first column tells me the name of each species group that I'll learn about. The next column shows the number of endangered species in the United States, and so on across the columns.

If I want to know how many birds in the United States are on the endangered species list, I would go to the second row labeled Birds and run my finger over to the Endangered U.S. column. There are 74 endangered species of birds in the United States.

If I want to know which plant or animal group in the United States is the most endangered, I run my finger down the Endangered U.S. column and find the largest number—551. Then I would run my finger back across the row until I found the name of the group— Flowering Plants.

(continued)

Guided Practice/Apply: Ask students to answer questions such as the ones that follow by using their charts:

1. *How many species of fish are endangered in the U.S.?* (69) *in foreign countries?* (11)

2. *Which plant or animal group needs the most protection in foreign countries?* (Mammals)

3. *Are reptiles more endangered in the U.S. or in foreign countries?* (in foreign countries)

4. *Why was this information included in the form of a chart?* (The chart shows the information more clearly than if it were written out. It also allows the reader to make comparisons more easily.)

Day 4: Identifying the Text Structure

Explain to students that they will reread the text to learn how the author organized it. The text structure of "Hanging By a Thread" is problem and solution. Point out to students that a text about a problem will very likely include some information that explains why the problem occurred (cause and effect) and that students should expect this. Use the Minilesson that follows.

Minilesson

Teaching the Text Structure: Problem and Solution

Introduce: Remind students that a writer of nonfiction organizes information in ways called text structures. The writer may:
- **compare and contrast** information,
- present information in a **sequence** of steps,
- put forth a **problem** and offer **solutions**,
- provide a detailed **description**,
- explain the **cause and effect** of an event.

Discuss the importance of identifying how text is structured. It alerts you to how the text was written. This knowledge can help you organize your thinking as you read.

Have students preview "Hanging By a Thread." Based on the title, introductory deck, and the headings, ask them to predict the text structure of the article (problem and solution).

Model: Use the Think Aloud on page 53 to model how you figured out the text structure.

Guided Practice/Apply: Have students reread the article. Distribute the graphic organizer for problem and solution, page 57. Ask them to fill it out as they read.

Day 5: Comprehension QuickCheck

After the lesson, you may use the following questions:

1. *What are some of the special features in this text? How do they help you?* (Answers should be based on the Reading Tools.)

2. *How did knowing the text structure help you?* (Answers may include: I remembered the information by noting each problem and its solution.)

3. *What new information did the chart provide about endangered species?* (Answers will vary.)

Independent Practice: Writing

Have students write a summary of the information they've just read. Suggest that they use the graphic organizer they completed while reading to help them create their summaries. Have them include the following:

- what the problem is in Hawaii,

- why the problem exists,

- what is being done about it.

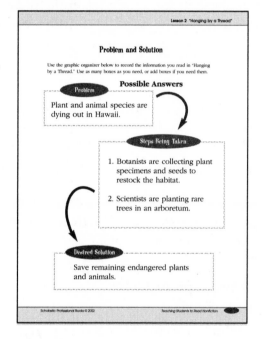

Lesson 2 "Hanging by a Thread"

Problem and Solution

Use the graphic organizer below to record the information you read in "Hanging by a Thread." Use as many boxes as you need, or add boxes if you need them.

Possible Answers

Problem

Plant and animal species are dying out in Hawaii.

Steps Being Taken

1. Botanists are collecting plant specimens and seeds to restock the habitat.

2. Scientists are planting rare trees in an arboretum.

Desired Solution

Save remaining endangered plants and animals.

Scholastic Professional Books © 2002   Teaching Students to Read Nonfiction

Web Links

www.exploratorium.edu/frogs   The Exploratorium's Frogs Exhibition

www.ran.org   Rainforest Action Network

animaldiversity.ummz.umich.edu/   University of Michigan
index.html

Think Aloud

The author of "Hanging By a Thread" has provided clues to the text structure of the article. The title means that someone or something is in a very insecure or shaky position. Hanging by a thread would certainly be a problem! The deck and the heading "Mass Destruction" tell me that the problem is that certain species in Hawaii are endangered. I think the author will probably explain what has caused the problem, too.

The next heading, "Saving What Remains," signals that the section will be about what people are doing to save the endangered species. That's a solution. From these clues, I can tell that the text structure is problem and solution.

Now I know what to expect as I read. This will help me understand the information and remember it.

Magazine Article

Most of us enjoy magazines of all kinds. Sports magazines, movie magazines, and computer magazines make for interesting reading. Most magazine articles are nonfiction. They contain information about subjects of special interest. Take, for example, an article in a science magazine. It is often about a timely topic of importance.

Even at first glance, you'll see how different a magazine article looks from a page in a story. For one thing, it's a lot busier. Several fonts are used, and they're in different sizes. There are also many features that are not found in novels. Magazine articles may include captioned photos, maps, charts, and other graphics. As in other kinds of nonfiction, these features are tools to help the reader better understand the information in the article. Of course, tools are only helpful if you know how to use them. Even a can opener won't do you any good if you don't know how it works.

Reading Tools

Use the tools below to help you read a magazine article.

- First **preview** the article. Use the features to figure out what you're going to read about.

- The **title** will tell you the topic of the article.

- Read the deck, or **introduction**, and the **headings** to find out the main ideas in the text. They are clues that let you know what to expect.

- Based on your preview, **predict** what you're going to read about.

- Now start to read the article. Words in **boldfaced type** signal important vocabulary that you'll need to remember. **Pronunciations** let you know how to say difficult words.

- Study the **graphic aids**. They may illustrate what's in the text or add new information.

- Read the **captions** carefully. They explain the graphic aid and often add information that was not in the text.

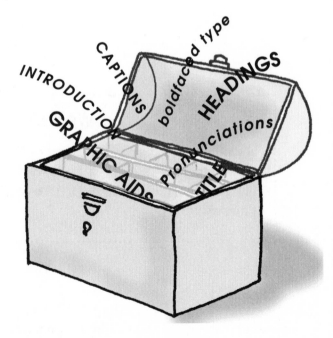

Remember to use the Reading Tools as you read "Hanging By a Thread."

Hanging
BY A Thread

Could Hawaii's vanishing species spell the end of paradise?

One morning last April, deep in the Alakai swamp on the Hawaiian island of Kauai, John Sincock and Jim Jacobi heard a sound that no one may ever hear again: a flutelike *oh-oh-oh*. The two scientists spotted the vocalist—a male Kauai o'o (OH-oh) bird. Sincock, a biologist at the U.S. Fish and Wildlife Service, had come with Jacobi, a botanist (a scientist who studies plants), to take pictures and record the calls of the very last o'o left in the world.

The o'o isn't the only creature vanishing in Hawaii. Of 71 known bird species, 26 have disappeared completely, and 31 are endangered—in immediate danger of extinction. Native plants are also in peril: about 120 of 1,000 flowering species have less than 20 individual plants left growing in the wild! Most of these species are victims of a brutal double-whammy: destruction of their native homes or habitats, and a steady onslaught of invader species, plants or animals imported from other countries that prey on native species or out-compete them for food or turf.

Paleontologists Helen James and Storrs Olson of the Smithsonian National Museum of Natural History study fossils of extinct Hawaiian species. They discovered that more than 50 bird species died out between 600 and 1800 A.D. As the Polynesian population grew, farms overtook lowlands, and the pigs and rats brought in by farmers trampled and devoured plants, snails, and other organisms. In the 19th century, an American ship imported two diseases to the islands: malaria, a disease spread by infected

Botanist Ken Wood rappels, or rope-climbs, down a cliff in Kauai, searching for endangered plants. Left, one of only three koki'o plants left in the world.

mosquitoes, and a bird virus called avian pox. Then residents introduced non-native songbirds and plants, which only further displaced local species.

Mass Destruction

Many biologists fear that Hawaii could be a grim indicator of the planet's future unless immediate actions are taken to halt mass species destruction. While the devastation is more gradual on Earth's continents than on many islands, scientists fear that half of all life forms on the planet could be extinct within a few thousand years. Even more alarming: "Earth will lose one fourth of all species in the next 30 years," claims Peter Raven, director of the Missouri Botanical Garden. In the world's rainforests, for example, 1 out of every 8 species is already near extinction.

Richard Stone © 2000. Adapted and reprinted with permission of *Discover* magazine

Saving What Remains

Steve Perlman, a botanist with the National Tropical Botanical Garden, rappels down cliffs and camps on mountaintops, risking his life to salvage rare Hawaiian plants. One place he works, the rugged Limahuli Valley in northwestern Kauai, is cut by deep ravines and plunging waterfalls. It's home to 10 endangered plant species, including the native Hawaiian palm tree and the last two cyanea shrubs in existence. Many plants have been choked out by a weed known as Koster's curse, brought to the island in the 1940s as an ornamental plant.

On a recent trip there, Perlman found a small, orange fruit hanging on a remaining cyanea— which could be the key to saving the species. He plucked the fruit and delivered it to the Lyon Arboretum in Honolulu, where the seeds can be coaxed to sprout. But Perlman won't be surprised if his "patient" doesn't make it.

Perlman and Ken Wood, another daredevil botanist, have racked up more than 1,000 expeditions over the last decade to collect rare plant specimens or save rare seeds. They hope to use these seeds to restock native habitats one day, but if there's no place to plant them, says Jacobi, "we might as well just snap nice pictures of them."

They and other environmentalists are battling to save remaining indigenous or native species. Scientists hope it's not too late.

Dozens of Hawaiian plants and animals face extinction, including Blackburn's hawkmoth (left).

Endangered and Threatened Species

GROUP	U.S. Endangered	FOREIGN Endangered	U.S. Threatened	FOREIGN Threatened	TOTAL
Mammals	61	248	8	16	333
Birds	74	178	15	6	273
Reptiles	14	65	22	14	115
Amphibians	9	8	8	1	26
Fishes	69	11	43	0	123
Insects	28	4	9	0	41
Flowering Plants	551	1	137	0	689

This chart shows the world's endangered and threatened animals and plants as of November 1999. An endangered species is in immediate peril of becoming extinct, while a threatened one is likely to become endangered without protection. *Source: U.S. Fish and Wildlife Service*

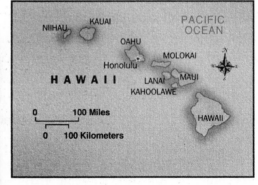

Ken Wood collects seeds from the pokalakala (poh-ka-LAH-ka-la) tree to plant in an arboretum. Only 50 of the trees remain in Kauai.

Teaching Students to Read Nonfiction

Problem and Solution

Use the graphic organizer below to record the information you read in "Hanging By a Thread." Use as many boxes as you need, or add boxes if you need them.

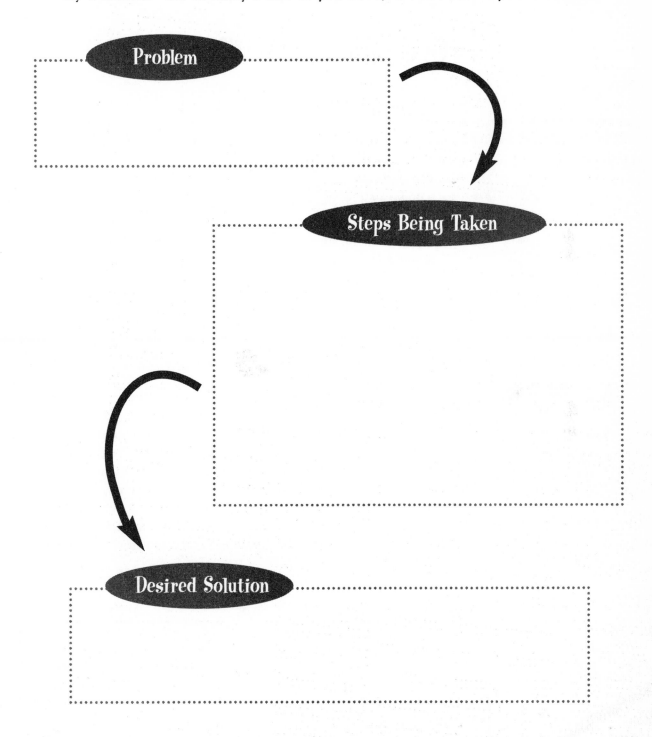

How to Read a Map

What Are Maps?

Help students understand that a map is a flat picture of Earth. There are five main types of maps: political, physical, landform, transportation, and historical.

- A *political map* shows information such as countries, states, cities, and capital cities.
- A *physical map* shows the Earth's natural features, such as mountains, oceans, and rivers.
- A *landform map* shows the shape of Earth's landmasses and bodies of water using colors and symbols.
- A *transportation map* shows how you can travel from one place to another.
- A *historical map* shows information about past events and places.

Materials

✳ Model Text, "About Florida," pp. 60–61

✳ Text Structure Transparency 6

✳ Bookmark, p. 159

Why Are They Useful?

Maps are a visual way to represent a great deal of information in a limited space. Therefore, maps often use symbols instead of words. For example, a map may show a particular landform using a color or type of line, such as cross-hatching. Or, a map might show a city using a small circle or dot with the city's name written beside it. A capital city might be represented by a star inside a circle to distinguish it from other cities. Maps can help you visualize a place as you read about it.

———————————— ✳ ————————————

Direct Instruction

- Distribute the Map lesson, pages 60–61. Have students read it silently before discussing the model text together. Then, display the *color transparency* and use it to guide students as they read and use the Reading Tools.
- Use the *Minilesson* to teach the text features.

Teaching the Text Feature

Introduce: Point out that a map contains clues that will help students read and understand it. To read maps, students should:

- Read the *map title*. It tells you what the map is about.

- Find the *symbols* on the map. A symbol is a picture or even a special color. It stands for a real thing or a real place.

- Look at the *map key* to learn what each symbol means.

- Read the *labels* on the map. They tell the names of geographical places.

- Find the map *scale*. The scale shows the relationship between distances shown on a map and the real distances. For example, one inch on a map may stand for 100 miles.

- Find the *compass rose*. It shows the directions on the map. *N* stands for north, *S* for south, *E* for east, and *W* for west.

Model: Use the Think Aloud at right to model the use of text features.

Guided Practice/Apply: Have students read "About Florida" on page 61 to learn about this large southern state. Ask them to retell the information in their own words. You may also ask:

1. *What bodies of water are in or around Florida?* (Gulf of Mexico, Atlantic Ocean, Biscayne Bay, Florida Bay)

2. *What cities are in southern Florida?* (Miami, Key Largo, Key West, Kendall)

3. *What is the capital city of Florida?* (Tallahassee)

4. *What large city is located northeast of St. Petersburg?* (Tampa) *About how far is it from St. Petersburg?* (Tampa is approximately 25 miles away.)

5. *What symbol is used to show Florida's highest point?* (a triangle)

Think Aloud

The title tells me that this map shows the state of Florida. Looking at the map key, I see that many map features are color-coded. For example, I see that the Gulf of Mexico and the Atlantic Ocean—two bodies of water—are in blue. Other bodies of water, such as bays and everglades are in blue, too.

I also see the major cities identified by a small dot with the city's name written beside it. Using the scale, I can estimate the distance from one city to another.

Comprehension QuickCheck

After you have completed the lesson, you may use the following questions to check students' comprehension:

1. *What is a map?* (a flat representation of a place)

2. *Why is a map helpful?* (It can show a large place in a very small space. It can also help you find places.)

3. *What does this map show?* (Florida)

4. *If you wanted to draw a map of your city, which map type would you choose? Why?* (Answers will vary, but should be supported.)

5. *If you had to tell a classmate why maps are useful, what would you say?* (Answers should reflect a clear understanding of maps and their uses.)

Map

A map is a flat picture of Earth. Imagine looking down on Earth from high in the sky. You would see the shapes of continents, large and small bodies of water, mountain ranges, and other natural features. There are five main types of maps: political, physical, landform, transportation, and historical.

- A **political map** shows information such as countries, states, cities, and capital cities. These maps are used to show the borders between large, organized areas.

- A **physical map** shows the Earth's natural features, such as mountains, oceans, and rivers. One type of physical map is the landform map.

- A **landform map** shows the shape of Earth's landmasses and bodies of water using colors and symbols. For example, bodies of water might be in blue and mountain ranges might be in various shades of brown to show elevation.

- A **transportation map** shows how you can travel from one place to another. Some transportation maps show major and minor roads that link cities and towns. Other transportation maps show bus, subway, train, boat, or airline routes.

- A **historical map** shows information about past events and places. These maps often show place names and political boundaries that differ from those today.

Reading Tools

In this lesson, you will be reading a political map. Use the Reading Tools below to help you read this type of map.

- Read the **map title**. It tells you what the map is about.

- Find the **symbols** on the map. A symbol is a picture or even a special color. It stands for a real thing or a real place.

- Look at the **map key** or **legend**. It tells you what each symbol on the map means.

- Read the **labels** on the map. These words tell the names of cities, states, countries, rivers, mountains, oceans, and other geographical places.

- Find the map **scale**. The scale shows the relationship between distances shown on a map and the real distances. For example, one inch on a map may stand for 100 miles.

- Find the **compass rose**. It shows the directions on the map. **N** stands for north, **S** stands for south, **E** stands for east, and **W** stands for west.

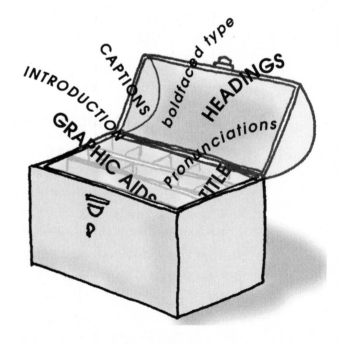

Remember to use these Reading Tools when you read a map.

Interstate Highways   State Capital   National Parks and Refuges   Marshlands   Highest Point

0   miles   50
0   kilometers   80

ABOUT FLORIDA

ALABAMA

GEORGIA

Albany

Dothan

Lake Seminole

Valdosta

Pensacola

Tallahassee

Jacksonville

Panama City

St. Augustine

ATLANTIC OCEAN

Gainesville

DID YOU KNOW?

that St. Augustine is the oldest continuously occupied European settlement in North America?

Lake George

Daytona Beach

Ocala

Orlando

Cape Canaveral

John F. Kennedy Space Center

GULF OF MEXICO

Melbourne

Tampa

Clearwater

Lakeland

Lake Kissimmee

Palm Bay

St. Petersburg

Sarasota

Port St. Lucie

Port Charlotte

Lake Okeechobee

West Palm Beach

Fort Myers

Coral Springs

Boca Raton

Pompano Beach

Naples

Fort Lauderdale

Hollywood

Hialeah

Miami Beach

Miami

Biscayne Bay

Kendall

Everglades National Park

Key Largo

Florida Bay

Florida Keys

Key West

Marathon

The most important industry in Florida is tourism. For many years, northern "snowbirds" have wintered in the Sunshine State. Now tourism flourishes during summer, too. Walt Disney World near Orlando, for example, is among the top five tourist attractions in the world.

◄———— **361 miles (581 km)** ————►

from *Scholastic Atlas of the United States*. Copyright © 2000 by Scholastic Inc.

61

Reading "Our Country's Landforms"

Build Background

Students will be viewing a landform map of the United States and reading information about the characteristics of each landform.

Create a blank Smart Chart and distribute copies, or create one on butcher paper. Use the routine on page 24. Through your questioning, guide the discussion to identify students' knowledge and/or misconceptions about landforms.

The gaps in students' prior knowledge should determine what of the following information to share.

- Landforms are different shapes of the surface of the land.
- The four main landforms are mountains, hills, plateaus, and plains.
- There are many different landforms in the United States.

Preteach Vocabulary

Materials

✳ Model Text, "Our Country's Landforms," pp. 66–67

✳ Graphic Organizer, p. 65

Knowledge Rating Chart

	Can Define	Know Some Information About	Don't Know
plateau			
canyon			
coastline			
interior			
landforms			

Preteach the following words from Our Country's Landforms using the Vocabulary Routine on page 29. Or you may wish to use the Knowledge Rating chart shown at left. After each student rates his or her knowledge of the words, follow up with a discussion of which words are the easiest, most difficult, most unfamiliar to the greatest number of students. Encourage students to share what they know about the words. The discussion will also give you an idea of how much knowledge students bring to the concepts they will be reading about.

Define each word. Be sure to point out unusual pronunciations, compound words, related words, and other aspects of the word.

- **plateau, canyon:** Focus on the unusual pronunciations of these words. Explain that the word *plateau* comes from French and the word *canyon* is derived from Spanish.
  plateau: high, flat tables of land
  canyon: very deep valleys with steep sides

- **landforms, coastline:** Point out that these words are compound words. Explain how knowing this can help students figure out the meaning of each word.
  landforms: different shapes of the surface of the land
  coastline: the strip of land where a body of water meets a land mass

- **interior**: Point out related words. For example, explain that while *interior* means "inside," *exterior* means "outside."
  interior: located within or inside something

Distribute copies of "Our Country's Landforms," pages 66–67. Have students preview the selection using the Preview Routine on page 41. Then, guide students as they apply the strategies they have learned for navigating text. Remind students to use the Reading Tools to read the map provided.

Before the second reading, use the Minilesson below to teach students about the selection's text structure: description.

Minilesson

Teaching the Text Structure: Description

Introduce: Discuss the importance of identifying how text is structured. It alerts readers to how the text was written. This can help them organize their thinking as they read. Tell students that a map presents information in a visual format using symbols and few words.

Model: You may wish to use the Think Aloud to model how to determine the text structure of "Our Country's Landforms."

Guided Practice/Apply: As students reread the selection, have them complete the graphic organizer for main idea/details, page 65. Then have students work in pairs to retell the information in their own words.

Think Aloud

Writers organize their writing in a way that helps us understand it. As I look at the U.S. Landforms map, I see a lot of details. The author has provided a description of each type of landform found in the United States. So, as I read this map I will try to remember the most important facts about each landform.

Comprehension QuickCheck

After you have completed the lesson, you may use the following questions to check students' comprehension:

1. In what states would you find plateaus? *(Washington, Oregon, Nevada, Utah, Arizona, New Mexico, Colorado, Wyoming, Montana, Kansas, Nebraska, Texas, Oklahoma)*
2. What is a canyon? *(a very deep valley with a steep side)*
3. What landform covers most of the United States? *(plains)*
4. Which landform covers your state? *(Answers will vary.)*
5. How can you show different landforms on a map? *(color, cross-hatching, or other art techniques)*

Independent Practice: Writing

Have students write a summary of the information they've just read. Suggest that they use the graphic organizer they completed while reading to help them create their summaries. Have them include the following:

- the names of the 4 major landforms found in the United States,
- the characteristics of each landform.

Possible Answers

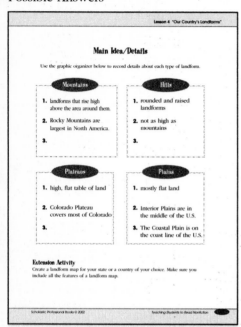

Web Links

www.mapquest.com	MapQuest
education.dot.gov/k5/gam5.htm	"Transportation Wonderland" from the U.S. Department of Transportation
www.nationalgeographic.com/maps	National Geographic Maps and Geography
www.nps.gov/yell	Yellowstone National Park
www.nps.gov	National Park Service
www.si.edu	Smithsonian Institution
www.3datlas.com	3D Atlas Online
www.field-guides.com	Virtual Field Trips
www.smm.org/greatestplaces	The Greatest Places Online
www.edu4kids.com/states	State Capitals, Birds, and Flags
www.50states.com	U.S. States
www.cr.nps.gov/catsig.htm	National Historic Sites
www.libs.uga.edu/darchive/hargrett/ maps/maps.html	Historical Maps

Main Idea/Details

Use the graphic organizer below to record details about each type of landform.

Mountains

1.

2.

3.

Hills

1.

2.

3.

Plateaus

1.

2.

3.

Plains

1.

2.

3.

Extension Activity

Create a landform map for your state or a country of your choice. Make sure you include all the features of a landform map.

Our Country's

Some landforms are borders between
Landforms also make a difference

Mountains are landforms that rise very high above the area around them. The Rocky Mountains are the largest mountain group in North America.

Plateaus are high, flat tables of land. The Colorado Plateau covers a lot of Colorado.

Canyons are very deep valleys with steep sides. The Grand Canyon is the largest canyon in the United States.

The Interior Plains stretch across the middle of the United States. Plains are mostly flat land.

WASHINGTON

Columbia River

OREGON

IDAHO

MONTANA

Yellowstone River

Missouri River

NORTH DAKOTA

MINNESOTA

SOUTH DAKOTA

WISCONSIN

Des Moines River

ROCKY

WYOMING

NEBRASKA

Raccoon River

IOWA

Platte River

Missouri River

Mississippi River

ILLIN

Great Salt Lake

NEVADA

UTAH

COLORADO

KANSAS

MISSOURI

Sacramento

e River

Colorado River

MOUNTAINS

PACIFIC OCEAN

CALIFORNIA

ARIZONA

NEW MEXICO

Gila River

Arkansas River

ARKANSAS

OKLAHOMA

Red River

MISSISS

TEXAS

Colorado River

Brazos River

LOUISIANA

Rio Grande

Pecos River

ALASKA

Tanana River

0   400
Miles

HAWAII

0   100
Miles

Gulf of Alaska

PACIFIC OCEAN

Landforms

regions and states.
in how people live.

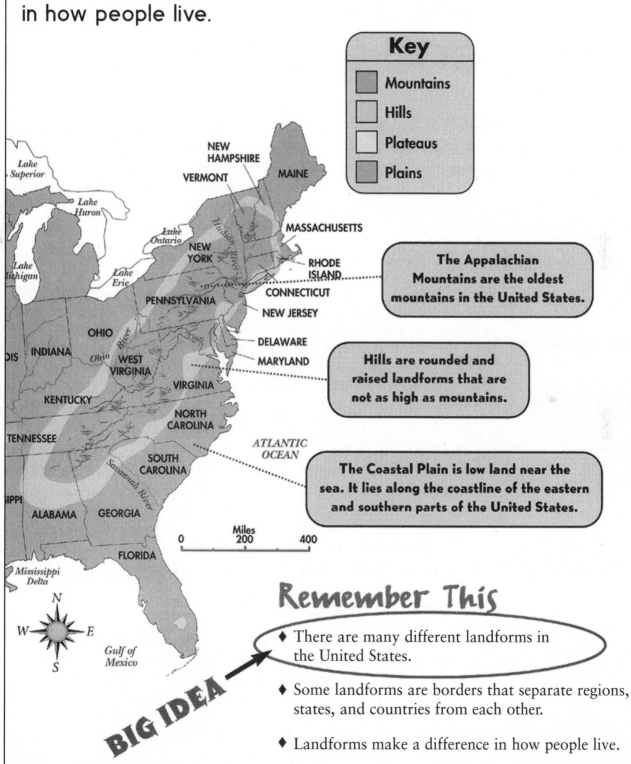

Key

- Mountains
- Hills
- Plateaus
- Plains

NEW HAMPSHIRE
VERMONT
MAINE
MASSACHUSETTS
NEW YORK
RHODE ISLAND
CONNECTICUT
PENNSYLVANIA
NEW JERSEY
OHIO
DELAWARE
INDIANA
MARYLAND
WEST VIRGINIA
VIRGINIA
KENTUCKY
NORTH CAROLINA
TENNESSEE
ATLANTIC OCEAN
SOUTH CAROLINA
ALABAMA
GEORGIA
FLORIDA
Mississippi Delta
Gulf of Mexico

Lake Superior
Lake Huron
Lake Ontario
Lake Michigan
Lake Erie
Hudson River
Ohio River
Savannah River

The Appalachian Mountains are the oldest mountains in the United States.

Hills are rounded and raised landforms that are not as high as mountains.

The Coastal Plain is low land near the sea. It lies along the coastline of the eastern and southern parts of the United States.

Miles
0   200   400

N
W   E
S

Remember This

♦ There are many different landforms in the United States.

♦ Some landforms are borders that separate regions, states, and countries from each other.

♦ Landforms make a difference in how people live.

BIG IDEA

How to Read Graphs

What Are Graphs?

A graph is a drawing used to represent numerical information. Students are most likely to encounter line graphs and circle, or pie, graphs in their content area reading. A *circle graph* illustrates how something can be divided into parts and shows how each part relates to the whole. A *line graph* shows how particular information has changed over time.

Why Are They Useful?

Graphs present numerical information in a condensed form that can be interpreted quickly and clearly. Knowing how to read and interpret a graph allows the reader to make comparisons and draw conclusions about the data. Graphs are found in periodicals, in nonfiction, and on TV when comparisons are being made about numerical information. Reading graphs is a skill that is useful throughout life.

---✳---

Materials

✳ Model Text, "Diversity in the United States," pp. 70–71

✳ Text Structure Transparency 7

✳ Bookmark, p. 159

Direct Instruction

- Distribute the Circle and Line Graphs lesson, pages 70–71. Have students read it silently before discussing the model text together. Then display the *color transparency* and use it to guide students as they read and use the Reading Tools.

- Use the *Minilesson* on page 69 to teach the text features.

Comprehension QuickCheck

You may use the questions below to check students' comprehension:

1. *What information does the line graph show that is not included in the circle graph? What information is shown in the circle graph and not in the line graph?* (The line graph shows how many people were immigrants, but does not tell where they were from. The circle graph shows the countries immigrants came from, but not when they came.)

2. *If you wanted to show the results of your weekly spelling tests for November, which graph would you choose?* (line graph)

3. *What type of graph would best show the kinds of things you spent your money on in the month of September?* (circle graph)

Minilesson

Teaching the Text Feature

Introduce: Explain that the two graphs present information about people in the United States. The line graph shows the foreign-born population of the United States in the last century. The circle graph shows the places immigrants originally came from.

To read the circle graph, students should follow the steps below.

- Read the *title*. It shows what the graph is about.

- Read the *labels*. The label on the left side of the graph tells you that the numbers represent the foreign born population of the United States. The numbers at the bottom are the years for which the population is given.

- Each *dot* stands for the population in a particular year. To find the population, put your finger on a dot. Trace from the dot to the side of the graph and read the number. Sometimes you have to estimate. To learn what year it was, trace from the dot down to the bottom of the graph.

- It is important to know that the line graph shows data only for the years that are given (1900, 1920, 1940, etc.). It does not include information about the 20 years in between each date, so you cannot make inferences about the population during that time. Therefore, the line connecting the dots does not mean that there was a steady increase during the intervening years; there may have been dips in some of the years.

Model: Use the Think Aloud to model the use of the Reading Tools.

Guided Practice/Apply: Have students read "Diversity in the United States" on page 71. You may wish to use the following questions to provide practice in reading the graphs:

1. *Which graph tells you when there were 14 million immigrants in the United States?* (line graph)

2. *Which graph tells you how many immigrants came from the Middle East? How many were there?* (circle graph; 1,035,000)

3. *In the circle graph, immigrants from Latin America represent about what part of the whole?* (about half)

4. *What was the foreign born population of the United States in 1960?* (about 10 million)

5. *What year had the greatest number of immigrants living in the United States?* (2000)

Think Aloud

Graphs give me information at a glance. For example, I can tell from a quick look at the line graph that the foreign born population of the United States increased between 1900 and 2000. I can learn more specific information, too. For example, there were approximately 11 million foreign born people in the United States in 1900.

From the circle graph I can tell that the largest number of immigrants living in the United States in 2000 originally came from Latin America. That section of the graph is the largest. I can learn more specific information, too. For example, the graph shows that 6,400,000 immigrants living in the U.S. in 2000 were originally from Asia.

Read About Social Studies

Circle and Line Graphs

When you read about a topic in social studies, you learn many facts. The facts often include numerical information such as how many hurricanes there were over the last 5 years or what the average teenager spends money on in a given month. It can be difficult to compare a lot of different numbers by reading them in a paragraph. Graphs can show the same information in ways that are quick and easy to read.

Graphs are diagrams that present numerical information in a visual way. You find graphs in books, magazines, newspapers, and on television.

- A **circle graph**, also called a pie graph, shows how something can be divided into parts or "slices" like a pie. It shows how each part fits into the whole. You can compare the parts with each other.

- A **line graph** shows change over time. You can trace the line of dots to see how the information in the graph has changed.

Reading Tools

In this lesson, you'll be reading an article that includes a circle graph and a line graph. Use the tools below to read them.

How to Read a Circle Graph

- Start by reading the **graph title**. It tells you what the whole graph represents.

- Each "slice" or **section** of the graph shows a part of the whole. You can see at a glance which section is the largest, which is the smallest, and which sections are in-between.

- The **label** tells what each section represents.

How to Read a Line Graph

- Read the **graph title**. It tells you what the line graph shows.

- Read the **labels** on the graph. They tell what each set of numbers represents.

- The **dots** in a line graph record an amount for a particular time.

- The dots are connected by a **line** which shows how something changed over time.

- To read a line graph, use your finger to **trace from the dot** to the number at the side and the time at the bottom.

- **Follow the line** to see how something increased or decreased.

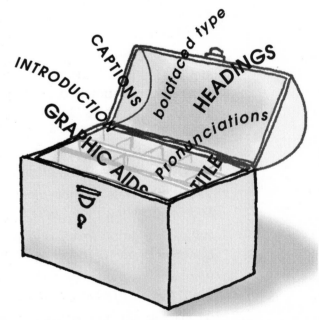

Remember to use these Reading Tools when you read graphs.

Diversity in the United States

Population Grows

The population of the United States more than tripled between 1900 and 2000. In those 100 years, millions of immigrants came to this country from Europe, Asia, Latin America, and Africa. Many immigrants from Latin America were escaping poverty or mistreatment because of their political views. Some immigrants, like Jews from eastern Europe, were escaping discrimination based on their religion. But all immigrants have come hoping to find a better life for themselves and their families in this country.

Changes in the immigration laws from 1965 to 1990 contributed to increased immigration. The foreign-born population in the United States grew from about 10 million in 1960, one of the lowest totals in the 20th century, to 14 million in 1980. By 2000, the foreign-born population in the United States was 28 million.

Greater Diversity

The changes in the immigration laws also allowed for greater diversity among the new arrivals. Between 1970 and 2000, the number of foreign-born residents from Europe dropped, and the number from Asia grew. The greatest growth during that time, however, was in the number of foreign-born residents from Latin America, which includes Central America and Mexico.

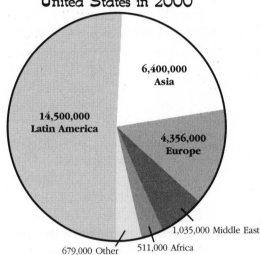

Origins of Immigrants in the United States in 2000

- 6,400,000 Asia
- 14,500,000 Latin America
- 4,356,000 Europe
- 1,035,000 Middle East
- 511,000 Africa
- 679,000 Other

Total: 27,481,000

Source: Center for Immigration Studies

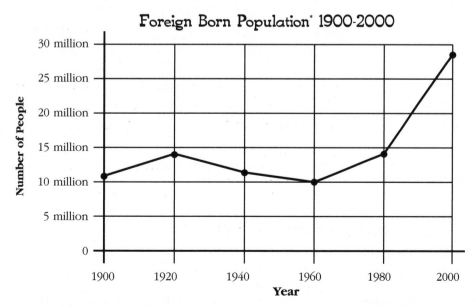

Foreign Born Population* 1900-2000

(Y-axis: Number of People — 0, 5 million, 10 million, 15 million, 20 million, 25 million, 30 million)

(X-axis: Year — 1900, 1920, 1940, 1960, 1980, 2000)

* Foreign born population refers to people who were not U.S. citizens at birth. Source: U.S. Census Bureau

Reading "Coming to America"

Build Background

Students will be reading about immigration to the United States during its peak, between 1880 and 1930. Create a blank Smart Chart and distribute copies or create one on butcher paper. Use the routine on page 24. Through your questioning, guide the discussion to identify students' knowledge and/or misconceptions about immigration in the early 1900s.

The gaps in students' prior knowledge will determine what of the following information you share prior to reading.

- More than 27 million immigrants entered the United States between 1880 and 1930. About 20 million of these immigrants passed through Ellis Island in New York harbor. Most of the arrivals were Europeans. During this time, the door was wide open for them.

- Asian immigrants had a very different experience. Chinese were the largest group of Asian immigrants. After the Civil War, Chinese workers were welcomed into the United States, primarily to work on the transcontinental railroad. But in the 1870s, the economic boom was ending. American workers viewed the Chinese immigrants as competition and a threat to their jobs. Congress passed the Chinese Exclusion Act in 1882, which barred all Chinese laborers from entering the country. Only students, merchants, tourists, and children of American citizens were allowed to enter.

- The Chinese Exclusion Act was the only legislation in American history to discriminate against a specific ethnic group. It was repealed in 1943, allowing Chinese immigration for the first time in 60 years.

Materials

✱ Model Text, "Coming to America," pp. 76–77
✱ Graphic Organizer, p. 75

Preteach Vocabulary

Preteach the words below from "Coming to America." Present each word and provide an example sentence. Define the word. Broaden students' associations to the word by pointing out affixes and related words.

- **majority:** more than half of the number in a group. The majority of students in my school ride the school bus. *Majority is related to the word major, meaning greater in size, number, or extent. Its opposite is minority.*

- **barracks:** large, very plain buildings that are often temporary housing for soldiers or workers. *The immigrants lived in crowded, uncomfortable, wooden barracks for weeks.*

- **detainees:** people who are kept confined or held back. *The detainees were held for questioning and were not allowed to enter the United States.*

  The word *detainee* is related to *detain* just as *employee* is related to *employ, standee* to *stand*, and *trainee* to *train*.

- **barriers:** things that block the way; obstructions. *The police put barriers around the building to protect it.*

Read the Selection

- Distribute copies of "Coming to America," pages 76–77. Have students preview the selection using the Preview Routine on page 41. Then guide students as they apply the strategies they have learned for navigating text. Remind students to use the Reading Tools to interpret the graphs.

- Before the second reading, use the Minilesson below to teach the text structure of the selection—compare and contrast.

Minilesson

Teaching the Text Structure: Compare and Contrast

Introduce: Discuss the importance of identifying how the text is structured. Remind students that figuring out how a selection is structured will help them organize their thinking as they read.

Model: You may wish to use the Think Aloud to model how to determine the text structure of "Coming to America."

Guided Practice/Apply: As students reread the selection, have them fill in the graphic organizer for compare and contrast, page 75. Then have half the class work in pairs to retell in their own words the information about Ellis Island and Angel Island in the early years. Ask the other half of the class to work in pairs to retell the information about the two immigration centers today.

Think Aloud

I know that writers organize their writing in a way that helps us better understand and remember the information. As I read the selection, I find the writer is comparing and contrasting the experiences of European immigrants coming to America through Ellis Island with the Asian immigrants who came through Angel Island. In the section about Angel Island, the writer says, "Immigrants there had a much more difficult time." That tells me that I'll learn about how the experiences were different.

The writer ends by describing Ellis Island today and Angel Island today. Again, I look for similarities and differences in the two places. When I'm finished reading, I understand what was the same and what was different about the experiences of European immigrants and Asian immigrants. I also know about the similarities and differences between Ellis Island and Angel Island today.

Comprehension QuickCheck

After you have completed the lesson, you may use the following questions to check students' comprehension:

1. *What text features were included in* Coming to America? *What was their purpose? How were they helpful?* (Answers should include: headings that outline the main ideas, boldfaced words that signal important vocabulary, and graphs that illustrate the numerical information.)

2. *What did a quick look at the line graph show you?* (Chinese immigration was at its peak in 1920, and then it dropped.)

3. *What did a quick look at the circle graph show you?* (Most immigrants in California in 2000 came from Latin America. The fewest came from Nigeria in Africa.)

4. *Were Asians the largest immigrant group in California in 2000?* (Asians were the second largest immigrant group in 2000.)

5. *What were some of the main differences between treatment of the immigrants entering through Ellis Island and those entering through Angel Island?* (Asians entering through Angel Island had a much more difficult time. There was prejudice against them, and they were detained far longer.)

Independent Practice: Writing

Imagine that you are entering the U.S. through Ellis Island or Angel Island in the early 1900s. Write a diary entry describing your experiences.

Possible Answers

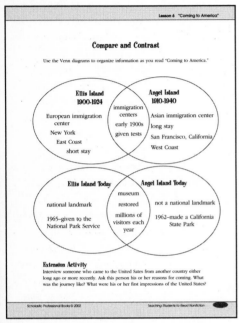

Web Links

www.americanhistory.si.edu	National Museum of American History
www.camla.org	The Chinese American Museum
www.nps.gov/stli	Statue of Liberty National Monument
www.ellisisland.org	Ellis Island
www.ushmm.org	U.S. Holocaust Memorial Museum
www.pbs.org/kcet/newamericans	"The New Americans" from PBS
www.aiisf.org	Angel Island Immigration Station Foundation

Compare and Contrast

Use the Venn diagrams to organize information as you read "Coming to America."

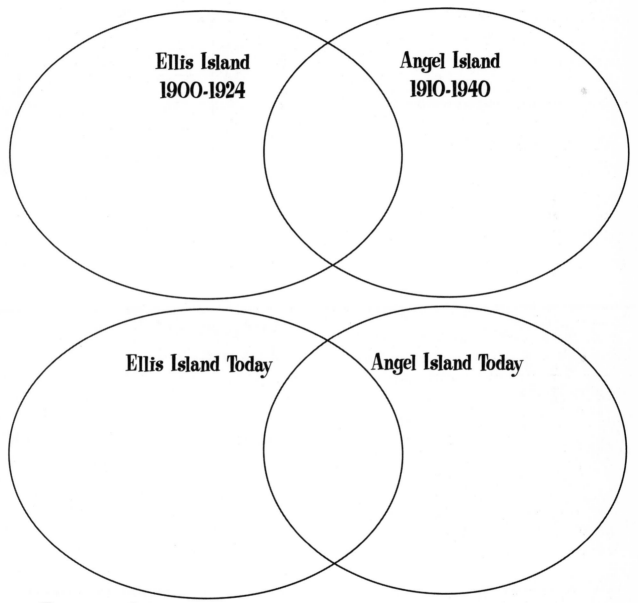

Extension Activity

Interview someone who came to the United Sates from another country either long ago or more recently. Ask this person his or her reasons for coming. What was the journey like? What were his or her first impressions of the United States?

Coming to America

United States has often been called a nation of immigrants. In 1920, 40% of the population were immigrants or the children of immigrants. In America's largest cities, the number was even higher with immigrants forming more than 70% of the population. Most were fleeing from poverty and starvation, religious persecution, and tyrannical governments. What they saw in America was freedom and the opportunity to make a better life for themselves and their families.

Welcome to Ellis Island

From 1850 to 1954, over 12 million immigrants from Europe entered the country. For most of them, Ellis Island in New York harbor was their first stop. Ellis Island was the main **immigration center** in the United States at that time. In the early years, between 1900 and 1924, thousands passed through Ellis Island daily. It is recorded that in one single day in 1907, 11,747 hopeful arrivals filed through the center.

Immigrants were required to pass a series of inspections before they could set foot on America's shores. Men, women, and children lined up in a huge room called the Great Hall as they waited to be examined by doctors and questioned by government officials. To determine whether the immigrants were healthy and mentally fit, they were

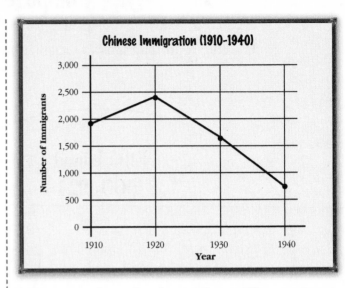

Chinese Immigration (1910-1940)

given many physical and mental tests. The experience was often nerve wracking. However, despite crowded and difficult conditions, the majority of immigrants made it through the battery of tests in a few hours, and they were allowed to enter the country.

Angel Island, the "Ellis Island of the West Coast"

At the same time immigrants from Europe were crossing the Atlantic, almost a million Asian immigrants were making the three-week trip across the Pacific Ocean. From 1910 to 1940, Asian immigrants entered the United States by way of Angel Island, located in San Francisco Bay. Angel Island was sometimes called "the Ellis Island of the West Coast," but immigrants there had a far more difficult time than the Europeans entering at Ellis Island. Officials at Angel Island were not welcoming to the Asians. They set up many barriers for Asian immigrants trying to enter. Immigrants faced extreme crowding, endless questioning, and days and days of waiting at the Angel Island Immigration Station. Those who were detained the longest were the Chinese, who often waited for weeks and even months.

The Chinese were the largest group to come from Asia. They had first begun to arrive in California in

1849 when news of the discovery of gold spread throughout the world. Like many other immigrants, they left lives of poverty to journey to what they called "Gold Mountain." Even after the hope of striking it rich faded, Chinese workers continued to flock to California for the opportunity to work on the building of the transcontinental railroad, which would run across the country and link the eastern part of the United States with the West. In 1869, when the last spike was hammered into place at Promontory Point in Utah, thousands of Chinese were left unemployed. Most of them made their way back to California, Washington, and Oregon where they found work on farms and orchards.

A Place to Wait

In later years, between 1910 and 1940, about 175,000 Chinese passed through Angel Island. Their first sight of a pleasant hillside with palm trees gave them no clue as to what awaited them. The buildings in which the immigrants were detained were wooden **barracks** surrounded by guard towers and barbed-wire fences with locked gates. Immigrants were separated by nationality and gender into crowded rooms. Husbands and wives were not allowed to see each other until both had been cleared to enter the country. Feeling like prisoners, many of the Chinese detainees expressed their sadness, anger, and pain by writing poems, which they carved on the wooden walls.

> There are tens of thousands of poems
> composed on these walls.
> They are all cries of complaint and sadness.
> The day I am rid of this prison and attain
> success,
> I must remember that this chapter once
> existed.
> — By One From Xiangshan (Poem 31)

Preserving History

Ellis Island closed in 1954 and was placed under the care of the National Park Service in 1965. Twenty years after that, work began on its **restoration**. The buildings

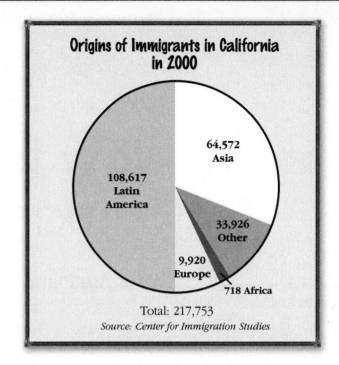

Origins of Immigrants in California in 2000

- 64,572 Asia
- 108,617 Latin America
- 33,926 Other
- 9,920 Europe
- 718 Africa

Total: 217,753
Source: Center for Immigration Studies

had been abandoned for so long that walls were crumbling, windows were broken, floors were rotting, and weeds were growing in the corridors. After eight years of careful and extensive rebuilding, the Ellis Island Immigration Museum opened to give visitors a first-hand look at the history of Ellis Island and the story of American immigration. Over 100 million Americans can trace ancestors to someone who passed through Ellis Island, so it is no surprise that the museum has almost two million visitors a year.

On the West Coast, a raging fire at Angel Island caused the station to be moved to San Francisco in 1941. The Island became a California State Park in 1962. Since then, people have worked to restore the buildings as a testimony to Asian immigrants. The wooden barracks, with their first-hand accounts carved on the walls, have already been restored and opened to visitors. About seventy-five percent of the Chinese and Japanese in California have their roots in Angel Island. They and many others hope that Angel Island will eventually be made a national landmark. People want Angel Island to be a center that preserves the history of Asian immigration, just as Ellis Island keeps the story of European immigration alive. Both places are an important part of America's past to be studied by all of us.

Sources: www.aiisf.org and internationalchannel.com

How to Read Primary Sources

What Are Primary Sources?

A primary source is an account of an event by someone who witnessed it. Letters, journals, photographs, interviews, newspaper accounts, and speeches are examples of primary sources. Sometimes you will find that a secondary source, such as a biography, includes primary source materials, such as photographs of and quotes by the person.

Why Are They Useful?

Primary sources are usually very informative because they reveal the thoughts and feelings of people who were "on the scene." They provide snapshots in time of how people lived and what they thought about the current events. Primary sources help to personalize historical events for the reader.

———————————— ✳ ————————————

Materials

✳ Model Text, "The Shirley Letters," pp. 80–81

✳ Text Structure Transparency 8

✳ Bookmark, p. 159

Direct Instruction

- Distribute the Primary Sources lesson, pages 80–81. Have students read it silently before discussing the model text together. Then, display the *color transparency* and use it to guide students as they read and use the Reading Tools.

- Use the Minilesson on page 79 to teach the text feature.

Comprehension QuickCheck

After you have completed the lesson, you may use the following questions to check students' comprehension:

1. *What are primary sources?* (firsthand accounts of an event written by a person who witnessed it)

2. *Why are primary sources helpful?* (They tell the thoughts and feelings of people who experienced an event.)

3. *What do these letters reveal?* (They tell what life was like for a doctor's wife in the California mines of the 1850s.)

4. *What primary source material do you encounter every day?* (Answers will vary, but may include newspapers, diaries, letters, e-mails, and so on.)

5. *If you had to tell a classmate about primary sources, what would you say?* (Answers should reflect a clear understanding of primary sources.)

Minilesson

Teaching the Text Feature

Introduce: Point out that primary sources are accounts of an event by someone who witnessed it. Letters, journals, photographs, interviews, newspaper accounts, and speeches are examples of primary sources. Many times, primary sources are embedded in secondary sources such as nonfiction books and biographies. To read a primary source embedded in a secondary source students should:

- First, read the *title*. It tells what the article is about.

- Before beginning, *preview* the text to learn about the topic. Look for and notice any primary source material, such as letters, photographs, quotes, and so on. Many times this material is set off in a special way, such as in italics.

- Read the *main article*—the secondary source material. Sometimes the primary source material is embedded in the article. Other times, the primary source is in the side columns. Read this material after you finish reading the main material. Think about how the primary source adds to the information provided in the main article.

- Read the *primary source* material. Pay attention to who wrote it and when. Notice the personal descriptions and reactions to the event. Students should ask themselves, "How does this information add to what I know about the topic?"

Model: You may wish to use the Think Aloud to model the use of Primary Sources.

Guided Practice/Apply: Have students reread "The Shirley Letters" on page 81 to experience firsthand accounts of the California Gold Rush. Ask them to retell the information in their own words. You may also wish to ask the following:

1. *When were the letters written?* (1851–1852)

2. *What important event was happening in the United States at that time?* (the California Gold Rush)

3. *Who wrote the letters?* (Mrs. Clappe)

4. *What was life like in the mines?* (difficult and dangerous)

5. *How was life different in the mines from life today?* (Answers will vary, but should reflect an understanding of the letters' contents.)

Think Aloud

The title tells me that this article will contain letters from the California Mines during the famous California Gold Rush. These letters were written during the early 1850s at the height of the Gold Rush. This was an important time in our country's history.

These letters will help me understand what it was like for someone living during that time. What did they think were their chances for finding gold? What did they feel about the Gold Rush? What was life really like for these people? These and other questions might be answered by the letters.

Primary Sources

Whenever you do research on a topic, you can consult many different types of reference sources: encyclopedias, periodicals, and Internet sites. Different reference sources offer different kinds of information and provide different viewpoints on a topic. The most common types of reference sources are encyclopedia articles, nonfiction books, biographies, and informational articles. These sources are known as secondary sources. A **secondary source** is an account of an event by someone who did not witness it.

On the other hand, letters and journals, photographs, interviews, newspaper accounts, and speeches are examples of primary sources. A **primary source** is an account of an event by someone who witnessed it. Primary sources are usually very informative because they reveal the thoughts and feelings of people who were "on the scene." Sometimes you will find that a secondary source, such as a biography, includes primary source materials, such as photographs of and quotes by the person.

Reading Tools

In this lesson, you will be reading an article about the famous California Gold Rush of the 1850s. Included in the article are letters written by people involved in this historic event. Use the Reading Tools below to help you read this type of primary source.

- First, read the **title**. It tells you what the article is about.

- Before you begin, **preview** the text to learn about the topic. Look for any primary source material, such as letters, photographs, quotes, and so on. Many times this material is set off in a special way, such as in italics.

- Read the **main article**—the secondary source material. Sometimes the primary source material is embedded in the article. Other times, the primary source is in the side columns. Read this material after you finish reading the main material.

- Read the **primary source** material. Pay attention to who wrote it and when. Think about the time period. Notice the personal descriptions and reactions to the event. Ask yourself, "How does this information add to what I know about the topic?"

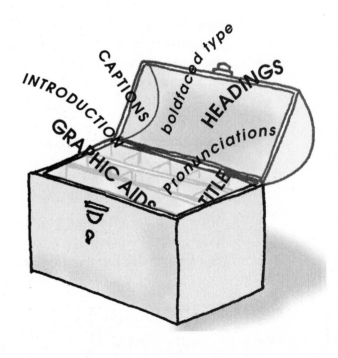

Remember to use these Reading Tools as you read primary sources.

The Shirley Letters

In 1849, the newlyweds Dr. and Mrs. Fayette Clappe left Massachusetts and set sail for California aboard the ship Manila. They settled in San Francisco, and Dr. Clappe opened an office. When the doctor fell ill in 1851, the couple moved to Feather River in the Sierra Nevada mountains because they believed the high altitude would help speed his recovery. Mrs. Clappe, who was now in her early 30s, wrote 23 letters to her sister in Massachusetts. In 1855, these letters, which form one of the best accounts of life in an early mining camp, were printed in Pioneer, *a California monthly magazine published in San Francisco. Mrs. Clappe chose not to use her real name—Louise Amelia Knapp Smith Clappe. Instead she used the pen name "Dame Shirley." Below is an excerpt from one letter:*

Letter the Seventh
From our Log Cabin, Indian Bar,
October 7, 1851
You will perchance be surprised, dear M. [author's sister], to receive a letter from me dated Indian instead of Rich bar, but as many of F.'s [author's husband] friends reside at this settlement, he concluded to build his log cabin here.

Solemn council was held upon the ways and means of getting "Dame Shirley" to her new home. The general opinion was, that she had better mount her fat mule and ride over the hill, as all agreed that it was very doubtful whether she would be able to cross the logs and jump the rocks which would bar her way by the water-passage…

It is impossible, my sister, to convey to you an idea of the wild grandeur and the awful magnificence of the scenery in this vicinity. This fork of the Feather River comes gliding along like a river in a dream, and anon bursting into a thousand glittering foam-beads over the huge rocks, which rise in its midst…. At every step golddiggers, or their operations, greet your vision, sometimes in the form of a dam, sometimes in that of a river turned slightly from its channel to aid the indefatigable [tireless] gold-hunters in their mining projects…,

The first thing which attracted my attention as my new home came in view, was the blended blue, red, and white of the American banner undulating like a many-colored snake amid the lofty…cedars which garland the brown brow of the hill behind our cabin. This flag was suspended on the Fourth of July last by a patriotic sailor, who climbed to the top of the tree to which he attached it, cutting away the branches as he descended, until it stood… a beautiful moss-wreathed liberty pole….

Enter…the room… is about twenty feet square. The fireplace is built of stones and mud, the chimney finished off with alternate layers of rough sticks and this same rude mortar. Contrary to the usual custom, it is built inside, as it was thought that arrangement would make the room more comfortable, and you may imagine the queer appearance of this unfinished pile of stones, mud, and sticks. The mantelpiece… is formed of a beam of wood, covered with strips of tin procured from cans, upon which still remain, in black hieroglyphics, the names of the different eatables which they formerly contained….

There, my dainty Lady Molly, I have given you… a description of my new home. How would you like to winter in such an abode? In a place where there are no newspapers, no churches, theaters; no fresh books; no shopping, calling… no parties… no daily mail… no vegetables but potatoes and onions, no milk, no eggs, no nothing? Now I expect to be very happy here.

Reading "The Monroe Family"

Build Background

Students will be reading an article about an early settler family during the California Gold Rush, combined with an interview of one of their descendants. Create a blank Smart Chart and distribute copies or create one on butcher paper. Use the routine on page 24. Through your questioning, guide the discussion to identify students' knowledge and/or misconceptions about the California Gold Rush.

If needed, share with students the following information prior to reading:

- Gold was discovered on January 4, 1848 at Sutter's Mill on the American River in northern California.

- The following year, the greatest gold rush in U.S. history began. Within two years, the population of California swelled from 14,000 to 100,000.

- Miners came from all across the United States and the world. The gold rush also drew merchants, artisans, and farmers to the region.

- The gold was originally found in the river in the form of dust, flakes, and nuggets. This supply was quickly exhausted and miners had to go to greater and more expensive lengths to find the gold.

Preteach Vocabulary

Preteach the following words from "The Monroe Family" using the Vocabulary Routine on page 29. Or you may wish to use the Word Connection Chart shown in the sidebar. Have students tell how each pair of words is related. Encourage students to use the words in a sentence. The discussion will also give you an idea of how much knowledge students bring to the concepts they will be reading about.

Define each word. Be sure to point out unusual pronunciations, related words, and other aspects of the word.

- **pioneer:** one of the first people to work or live in a new or unknown area. Focus on pronunciation. Point out the open syllable

Materials

✻ Model Text, "The Monroe Family," pp. 86–87

✻ Graphic Organizer, p. 85

Word Connection

Write each pair of words on the chalkboard. Have students discuss how the words are related.

pioneer .... panning

descendant .... pioneer

heirs .... inherited

descendant .... heirs

at the beginning of the word: *pi-o-neer*. Remind students that an open syllable ends in a vowel and has a long vowel sound.

- **descendant:** your children, their children, and so on in the future. Focus on related words: *descend, descending, descent.*

- **inherited:** received money, property, or other possessions from someone who has died. Focus on related words: *inherit, inheritance.*

- **heirs:** people who have been left money, property, or other possessions as a result of a will/death of a relative. Focus on the pronunciation of the word, specifically the silent *h,* as well as the related words *heiress* and *heirloom.*

- **panning:** looking for gold by washing earth in a pan or sieve. Focus on the other meanings of the word *pan*—(1) a wide, shallow container used for cooking; (2) to move a camera over a wide area in order to follow the action; (3) to harshly criticize someone or something.

Read the Selection

- Distribute copies of "The Monroe Family," pages 86–87. Have students preview the selection using the Preview Routine on page 41. Then, guide students as they apply the strategies they have learned for navigating text. Remind students to use the Reading Tools to read the article provided.

- Before the second reading, use the Minilesson below to teach students about the selection's text structure: sequence.

Minilesson

Teaching the Text Structure: Sequence

Introduce: Discuss the importance of identifying how text is structured. It alerts readers to how the text was written and can help them organize their thinking as they read. Tell students that an historical article is often written in the order in which events happened, in sequence.

Model: Use the following Think Aloud as you model how to determine the text structure of "The Monroe Family."

Guided Practice/Apply: As students reread the selection, have them complete the graphic organizer for sequence, page 85. Then have students work in pairs to retell the information in their own words.

Think Aloud

Writers organize their writing in a way that helps us understand it. I see that the article "The Monroe Family" presents information in a sequence. Each paragraph contains dates detailing important events in the lives of Nancy Gooch and her descendants.

The dates are written in chronological order to help me follow the sequence of events that happened to the family after they moved to California in 1850. Therefore, I know that the text structure is sequence.

Comprehension QuickCheck

After you have completed the lesson, you may use the following questions to check students' comprehension:

1. *Why was Nancy Gooch given her freedom in 1850?* (California became a U.S. state and entered as a free state, meaning no slaves were allowed.)

2. *What did the family do to earn money?* (They grew crops.)

3. *Why was their land so important?* (They owned the land where gold was originally discovered in California, thereby causing the famous Gold Rush in the mid-1800s.)

4. *Who is Evelyn Green?* (She is a descendant of Nancy Gooch.)

5. *How did the interview with her add to your understanding of this family and their historical importance?* (Answers will vary.)

Independent Practice: Writing

Have students write a summary of the information they've just read. Suggest that they use the graphic organizer they completed while reading to help them create their summaries. Have them include the following:

- the events in the order in which they happened to Nancy Gooch and her descendants after she moved to California,

- why this family is remembered today,

- how the interview adds to our understanding of this family.

Possible Answers

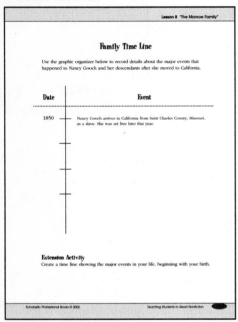

Web Links

www.si.edu/postal	National Postal Museum
www.undergroundrailroad.org	National Underground Railroad Freedom Center
www.law.ou.edu/hist	U.S. Historical Documents

Family Time Line

Use the graphic organizer below to record details about the major events that happened to Nancy Gooch and her descendants after she moved to California.

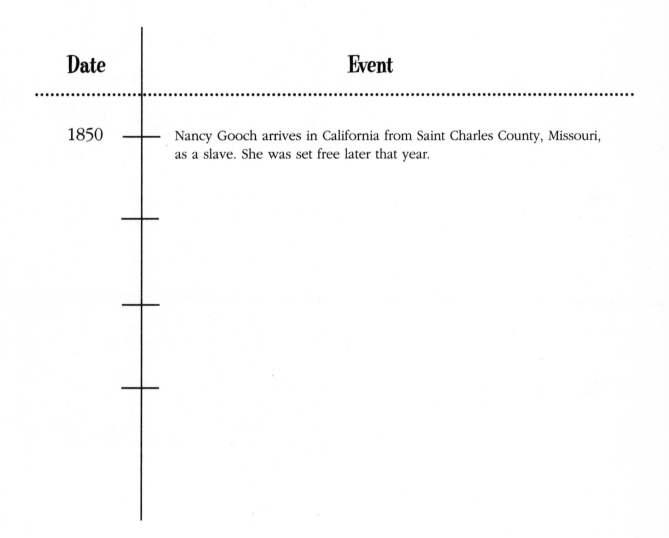

Date   **Event**

1850 ——— Nancy Gooch arrives in California from Saint Charles County, Missouri, as a slave. She was set free later that year.

Extension Activity

Create a time line showing the major events in your life, beginning with your birth.

The Monroe Family

BY OSBORNE WEST

"The old town has changed a lot since my time, but the land is still the same." These were the words of James (Jim) Monroe, grandson of Nancy Gooch. Jim was referring to Coloma, California, where in 1848, gold was discovered at John Sutter's mill. Jim's grandmother and her family were one of the three black pioneer families to settle in the town.

Nancy Gooch arrived in California in 1850 from Saint Charles County, Missouri. She came as a slave, but was given her freedom later that same year when California entered the union of the United States as a "free" state. Nancy worked hard, cooking and doing laundry for the miners. When she had saved $700, she sent the money to Missouri to buy her son Andrew's freedom. Andrew arrived in Coloma in 1870 with his wife, Sarah Ellen, and their two sons, Pearly (also spelled Pearley) and Grant. Jim was born in Coloma, along with the rest of his brothers and sisters—Garfield, William, Cordelia, and Andrew.

Jim's father grew apples and pears, as well as garden crops, to sell in the nearby communities. Gradually the Monroe family holdings grew from 80 acres to 360 acres. Their land included the gold discovery site.

When Jim's father died in 1920, his older brother Pearly inherited the land. In 1942, the site of Sutter's sawmill was purchased by the State of California Department of Parks and Recreation for use as a park—the Marshall Gold Discovery State Historic Park. Pearly learned to farm the rest of the property until he sold it to the state in 1963.

When Pearly died the following year, he left $125,000 to the National Association for the Advancement of Colored People (NAACP). In his will, he also included 35 children from the Coloma area as heirs. Today, the gravesite of the

This photo of Nancy Gooch and her husband was taken in San Francisco in the late 1800s.

Gooch family from Grandma Nancy to Jim is in the Coloma Pioneer Cemetery.

Osborne West *is a park maintenance worker at the Marshall Gold Discovery State Historic Park. He has researched and developed impressions of Jim Monroe and Pearly Monroe, and takes the role of each on special days, such as "Christmas in Coloma" and "Gold Discovery Days."*

from *Footsteps: African American History*, January/February 2001

Descendants

AN INTERVIEW WITH EVELYN GREEN *By Vicki Hambleton*

Evelyn Green is a descendant of Nancy Gooch. The mother of two grown children, she lives in Sacramento, California. But she spent much of her young life living at the family ranch in Coloma that today is the Marshall Gold Discovery State Historic Park. She told us of her memories of Coloma.

HOW ARE YOU RELATED TO NANCY GOOCH AND HER FAMILY?

Evelyn Green: *Pearly Munroe, who was Nancy Gooch's grandson, was my step-grandfather. He and my grandmother raised me. I lived with them from a very young age. My stepfather was a boxer and my mother traveled with him on the road, so I lived with my grandparents.*

HOW DID YOUR GRANDFATHER COME TO LIVE IN COLOMA?

Evelyn Green: *Perly inherited the ranch from his father. He lived his whole life there really. He came from Missouri with his parents at a young age, traveling across the country by covered wagon. He lived in Coloma full-time until he was older and married. Then, when I lived with him, we spent the week in Sacramento and traveled to Coloma every weekend.*

WHAT ARE YOUR MEMORIES OF YOUR CHILDHOOD WITH PEARLY?

Evelyn Green: *Well, first of all I have to say that everyone thought he was the kindest man. Every time he went to the grocery store, he would come home with a big*

bag of candy just for me. And he loved the earth.

The ranch was really his life, his home. He loved the environment. Even when we were in Sacramento, we had a huge garden of vegetables and flowers.

WAS FARMING IMPORTANT TO HIM?

Evelyn Green: *Oh yes, as I say, it was his life. I remember my grandfather had orchards, and fir trees, and vegetables. I never knew, until I was a teenager, that everybody didn't have a six-foot Christmas tree! At Christmas, he would go out and cut dozens of trees and bring them to family and friends. I also didn't know until I was much older that people bought fruit in the market, because we always had everything right there at the ranch—peaches, persimmons, pears. You name it, we grew it!*

DID YOUR GRANDFATHER EVER MINE FOR GOLD?

Evelyn Green: *Well, let me put it this way—at the time everyone in Coloma did some panning, but he never got involved seriously. He*

found some little specks—although to my child's eye, they didn't look like specks, but his interest was in the land and developing it for farming.

HOW LONG DID YOU LIVE AT THE RANCH?

Evelyn Green: *Well, I lived with my grandparents until I was a grown woman. Then my grandfather sold the property to the state in 1963. He died a year later. He was a wonderful man, and really I think the Munroe family was a wonderful family, because they contributed so much to the community and to the history of the area.*

The 1800s photo on the park's visitors' brochure shows Jim Monroe as a child (in white outfit).

How to Read Reference Sources

What are Reference Sources?

Reference sources are books or non-print media that contain factual information. A reference source may be an encyclopedia, almanac, atlas, newspaper, magazine, audio- or videocassette, computer database, or CD-ROM. Students will use reference sources when they write research reports.

- An *encyclopedia* contains general information about important people, places, objects, and events. Today encyclopedias are available on the Internet and CD-ROM in addition to print. An encyclopedia may be the first source students use to get an overview of a topic.

- *Nonfiction* includes biographies and autobiographies, and informational books about particular topics.

- *Periodicals* are newspapers and magazines. They contain articles that can provide the most recent facts about a topic.

- The *Internet* provides access to a vast number of sources of information—libraries, government agencies, media organizations, foundations, and museums, to list just a few.

Why Are They Useful?

The variety of reference sources that are available ensures that students will be able to find the kind of information they need in the most efficient way. To do this, of course, students will have to be familiar with different types of reference sources, the organization of each source, how to use it, and the research tasks for which each one is most suitable. Students should understand that they will find the information they are looking for more easily if they choose the appropriate reference source. They will save time, as well.

—————————— ✳ ——————————

Direct Instruction

- Distribute the Reference Sources lesson, pages 90–91. Have students read it silently before discussing the model text together.

Materials

✳ Model Text, "Blizzard Warning!" p. 91

✳ Text Structure Transparency 9

✳ Bookmark, p. 159

Then, display the *color transparency* and use it to guide students as they read and use the Reading Tools.

- Use the Minilesson below to model how to use reference sources.

Minilesson

Teaching the Text Feature

Introduce: Point out to students that when they are writing a research report, they will have gone through several steps before they use a reference source. They will have chosen a topic, narrowed it, and decided on the purpose and audience for their writing. After they have completed these steps, they are ready to begin their research.

Tell students that they will find the information they need more easily if they choose the appropriate reference sources. They will also save time, by not searching in the wrong sources.

Explain how students should use a nonfiction book as a resource.

- Look in the table of contents or the index to find out which pages have information about a particular topic (e.g., the Pony Express in a book about the Old West).

- To read the material, they should use the strategies they have learned for reading informational text.

Model: Use the Think Aloud at right to model how to use features of reference sources.

Guided Practice/Apply: Help students identify the part of the text that is a secondary source and the parts that are primary sources. Then have them compare the information they learned from each source.

Think Aloud

Imagine I am writing a report about snowstorms and blizzards. I have found a good reference source—a book about weather. I looked in the index to find the pages about blizzards.

When I turn to those pages, I preview the text and notice many features that I have seen before— a chapter title, headings, primary sources, and boldfaced words. So I read the title and headings to learn the main ideas in the chapter. Then I read the text, making sure I remember the boldfaced word.

The primary sources include two photographs and a memoir. One of the photos was taken 100 years before the other. It's interesting to see what's the same and what's different about them. The memoir makes the information in the text real to me.

Comprehension QuickCheck

After you have completed the lesson, you may use the following questions to check students' comprehension:

1. *What makes a snowstorm a blizzard?* (In addition to falling or blowing snow, there must be 35-mile an hour winds, visibility of 1/4 mile or less for at least three hours, and temperatures below 32 degrees.)

2. *What does the memoir contribute to your understanding?* (It shows the dangers and the effects of a blizzard on real people; reading the feelings of a person caught in a blizzard makes the ordeal real.)

3. *Even though the photographs were taken more that 100 years apart, what has not changed?* (There are still major blizzards; We are able to track storms today and make better predictions about the weather, but we can't control it.)

Reference Sources

Imagine that you have a homework assignment to write a report. Before you can begin, you have to do research about the topic you have chosen. Where would you look for the information you need? You would look in **reference sources**. Encyclopedias, books of nonfiction, and Internet Web sites are sources that contain information about many different topics.

An **encyclopedia** gives you general information about important people, places, things, and events. An encyclopedia may be a set of books, or it may be stored on a CD-ROM.

Nonfiction books provide in-depth information.

Articles in recent **periodicals** supply the most up-to-date information about a topic.

The **Internet** allows you to access many sources of information from a computer. Many government departments, museums, other organizations, and newspapers have sites that you can go to for information.

A reference source is not meant to be read through from cover to cover. You have to locate the part of the book that contains the information about your topic. For example, let's say you are writing a report about wolf packs, and you have a book about the wild animals of North America. You would look in the table of contents or the index to find the pages about wolves.

Reading Tools

In this lesson, you will be reading a section of a reference book about blizzards. When reading reference sources, use the Reading Tools below to help you.

- Look in the **table of contents** or the **index** to find the pages related to your topic.

- **Preview** the text as you would do with any nonfiction. Pay attention to the chapter title and headings.

- Then **read the text** to learn about your topic. Attend to any special features, such as boldfaced words, maps, diagrams, photographs, and so on.

- Look for **primary source** material. A primary source reveals the thoughts and feelings of a person who was on the scene.

- If the text includes **photographs**, study them carefully. Photographs are a primary source that can provide details and additional information about a topic. Be sure to read the captions, as well.

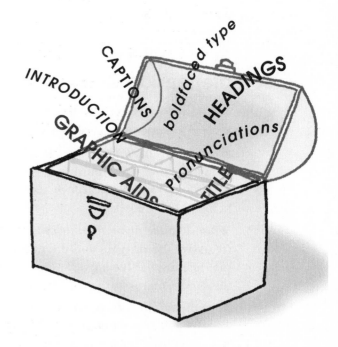

Remember to use these Reading Tools when you read a reference source.

Blizzard Warning!

Snow Plus Wind

Although many people use the term "blizzard" to describe any weather with a lot of snow, blizzards are really a special type of storm. In a true **blizzard**, the combination of falling and/or blowing snow plus sustained winds or frequent gusts of at least thirty-five miles an hour must lower the visibility to 1/4 mile or less for at least three hours in a row. Temperatures well below thirty-two degrees are typically associated with blizzards, too.

Snow Blowers

Strangely enough, blizzard conditions can occur without any snow actually falling from the sky. Strong winds can blow previously dumped snow, reducing the visibility to create blizzard conditions. Antarctica, which has some of the worst blizzards in the world, actually only gets a few inches of snow each year. But incredibly cold temperatures mean the snow never melts. So when the wind blows, it's stirring up years' worth of old snow.

A tunnel dug through the snow in Farmington, Connecticut, after the blizzard of 1888.

Snowbanks reach 116 inches in Moorhead, Minnesota, after winter storms in 1997 (right).

In the winter of 1888, a fifteen-year-old boy, O. W. Meier, and his two younger brothers battled a blizzard in Lincoln, Nebraska. Many years later, Mr. Meier still remembered that storm.

Beautiful big white flakes were falling fast that morning of the fateful day. At the last recess, the snow was about two feet deep. As swiftly as lightning, the storm struck the north side of the schoolhouse. The whole building shivered and quaked.

In an instant the room became black as night. The teacher said, "Those who live south may put on their coats and go, but the rest of you must stay here in this house."

We had not gone 16 feet when we found ourselves in a heavy drift of snow. We took hold of each other's hands [and] pulled ourselves out. The cold north wind blew us a half mile south. My brothers and I could not walk through the deep snow in the road, so we walked down the rows of corn stalks to keep from losing ourselves till we reached our pasture fence....

For nearly a mile we followed the fence till we reached the corral and pens. The roaring wind and stifling snow blinded us so that we had to feel through the yard to the door of our house. Pa was shaking the ice and snow from his coat and boots. He had gone out to meet us but was forced back by the storm.

That was an awful night on the open Plains. Many teachers and school children lost their lives in that blinding storm, while trying to find their way home. The blizzard of 1888 has not been forgotten.

— from American Life Histories: Manuscripts from the Federal Writers' Project, 1936–1940

Reading "Black Blizzard"

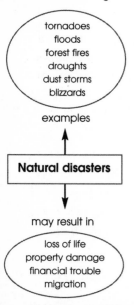

Materials

✳ Model Text, "Black Blizzard," pp. 96–97

✳ Graphic Organizer, p. 95

Concept Map

Draw a concept map for "natural disasters" on the chalkboard. Ask students to fill in the links using their prior knowledge and the vocabulary words. After students finish the selection, you may wish to come back to the map so that they can add new concepts based on their reading.

Possible answers are given.

> tornadoes
> floods
> forest fires
> droughts
> dust storms
> blizzards
>
> examples
>
> ↑
>
> **Natural disasters**
>
> ↓
>
> may result in
>
> loss of life
> property damage
> financial trouble
> migration

Build Background

Students will be reading a magazine article about the Dust Bowl. Create a blank Smart Chart and distribute copies or create one on butcher paper. Use the routine on page 24. Through your questioning, guide the discussion to identify students' knowledge and/or misconceptions about droughts in general and the Dust Bowl in particular.

The gaps in your students' prior knowledge should determine what of the following information you should share with them before they begin reading:

- In 1929, the United States entered a period known as the Great Depression. All across the country, businesses, factories, and banks shut down. People lost their savings. Many farmers went broke and lost their farms. Millions of people—one out of four—were out of work.

- Current maps do not include the old Route 66, because today most of it is closed or in disrepair. But at one time it was known as "The Mother Road" and "The Main Street of America." In the 1930s, people leaving Oklahoma to escape the Dust Bowl endured many hardships as they traveled nearly 2000 miles on Route 66, going through Texas, New Mexico, and Arizona to California where the road ended. The trip took from three weeks to six months and was made in cars and trucks that were loaded down with whole families and whatever goods they still possessed.

- "Okies" became a term of abuse used by many in California. However, it is what the people from Oklahoma called themselves, and to them the word meant pride, courage, and the determination to face hardships and overcome them.

Preteach Vocabulary

Preteach the following words from "Black Blizzard" using the Vocabulary Routine on page 29. Or you may wish to use the concept map shown in the sidebar.

Present each word and provide a context sentence. Define the word. Broaden students' associations to the word by pointing out pronunciations, when necessary, and related words.

- **migration:** movement from one region to settle in another. *The promise of free farmland led to a migration of thousands of people from the East to the West in the 1800s.* Relate *migration* to *migrate* (to move from one region to settle in another) and *migrant* (one who moves from one region to settle in another). *Migrant workers are people who move regularly from place to place.*

- **drought:** a lack of rain for a long period of time. *People were not allowed to water their lawns, all fountains were shut off, and public swimming pools were closed because of the drought.* Point out the pronunciation; *drought* rhymes with *out*.

- **mortgage:** the use of property as security against a loan. *The family took a mortgage from the bank to buy a farm. The family used their farm as a mortgage to buy the new machinery they needed.* Point out the silent *t* in *mortgage*.

- **impoverished:** made poor. *Many store owners were impoverished by the earthquake.* Point out the related word *poverty*.

Read the Selection

- Distribute copies of "Black Blizzard," pages 96–97. Have students preview the selection using the Preview Routine on page 41. Remind students to use the Reading Tools for reference sources.

- Before the second reading, use the Minilesson below to teach students about the selection's text structure: cause and effect.

Minilesson

Teaching the Text Structure: Cause and Effect

Introduce: Discuss with students the importance of identifying how text is structured. Remind students that figuring out how a selection is structured will help them organize their thinking as they read.

Model: You may wish to use the Think Aloud to model how to determine the text structure of "Black Blizzard."

Guided Practice/Apply: As students reread, help them complete the graphic organizer on page 95, showing the causes and effects of the drought in the 1930s. Then have students work with a partner to explain orally the information in the organizer, adding appropriate details.

Think Aloud

The writer begins by describing what a dust storm is like. The writer goes on to describe the effects of the dust storms that took place in the 1930s. Then the writer asks, "How did it happen?" That tells me I'm going to read about the causes of the dust storms and the migration. So as I continue to read, I'll look for causes and effects.

Making a graphic organizer that shows cause and effect will help me remember what happened and why.

Comprehension QuickCheck

After you have completed the lesson, you may use the following questions to check students' comprehension.

1. *How did knowing the text structure of "Black Blizzard" help you?* (Answers should include: Knowing the text structure helped me look for causes and effects of the dust storms as I read.)

2. *Why was the Dust Bowl so badly hit by the drought in the 1930s?* (The area was mostly wild grasses which held the soil together. The grasses were destroyed by the crops that farmers planted. When the crops dried up from lack of rain, there was nothing to hold the soil together, and it was blown away by the heavy winds.)

3. *Did the Okies find the better life they hoped for in the West? Explain.* (No, most of the Okies did not find a better life. There were not enough jobs in the West because of the depression, and so native Californians did not want competition from the newcomers. Also, most of the Okies could not afford decent housing, and were forced to live in camps under very harsh conditions.)

4. *Why was a dust storm called a "black blizzard?"* (Like a blizzard, a dust storm blows and blots out the sky and the landscape; but instead of being white snow that's blowing, it's black dust and dirt.)

5. *What did the primary source accounts add to your understanding?* (I learned details about the hardships and feelings from the migrants themselves.)

Independent Practice: Writing

Have students write a summary of the information they read in "Black Blizzard." Suggest that they use the graphic organizers they completed while reading to help them create part of their summaries. Tell students to include the following facts:

- what the Dust Bowl was,
- how it happened,
- what its effects were.

Possible Answers

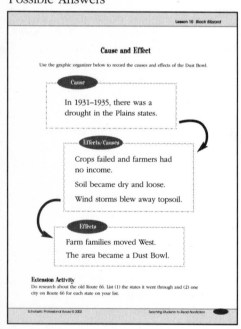

Web Links

www.wildweather.com   Dan's Wild Weather Page

www.exploratorium.edu   The Exploratorium

kidscience.about.com   Kid Science

Cause and Effect

Use the graphic organizer below to record the causes and effects of the Dust Bowl.

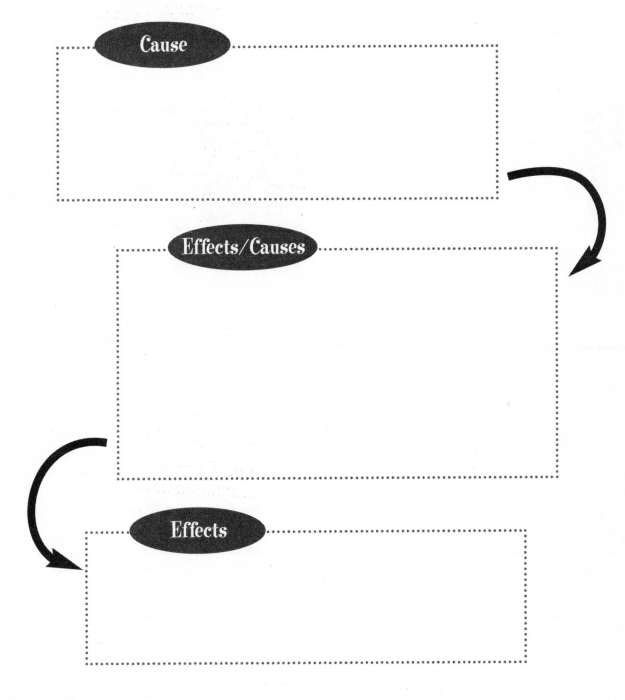

Extension Activity

Do research about the old Route 66. List (1) the states it went through and (2) one city on Route 66 for each state on your list.

Black Blizzard

THE DUST BOWL WAS ONE OF THE WORST NATURAL DISASTERS IN AMERICAN HISTORY. WHAT WAS IT, AND HOW DID IT HAPPEN?

Imagine this: You're eating breakfast one Tuesday morning, minding your own business. You chance to look out the window.

"Ma! Dad!" you yell. "It's back. Take cover!" Even though it's nine A.M., the sky in the distance is pitch black. A dry tidal wave of dust and dirt — 7,000 feet high — is rolling, howling towards you. Your parents race to cram wet towels in the spaces under doors and windows, as the huge black cloud rumbles closer.

It's an eerie sight. In front of the cloud, birds fly and rabbits run, terrified. Soon the cloud is here. The sky is pure black. The wind is screaming, pelting your tiny house with dirt. Your mom hands you a wet towel, which you put over your face, but you can still taste the dust, feel it with every breath, gritty between your teeth. You huddle in the middle of the room with your family in the total darkness, and wait for the dust storm to end.

A NATURAL DISASTER

In the mid 1930s, large areas of Oklahoma, Texas, Kansas, New Mexico, and Colorado were hit by hundreds of these storms. Together, the storms made up one of the worst natural disasters in America's history.

The dust storms destroyed the land, ruined the economy of the whole area, and threatened the lives of most of the population. Everyone who could, picked up and moved west. It became the greatest peacetime migration ever in America. How did it happen?

From 1900 to 1930, many families bought or leased small parcels of land in the Plains states, and built farms. The area was mostly dry grasslands, where

March 1936: A dust storm rises over the Texas Panhandle. Horace Ray Conley of Foss, Oklahoma, said storms like these made the sky "boil red, blood red."

crops are difficult to grow. With hard work, the farmers were able to grow wheat and corn, and to raise cattle.

But in 1931, a terrible drought fell across the middle of the nation. America was already suffering from the stock market crash of 1929 and the Great Depression. Now, from 1931 to 1935, the farmers got almost no rain at all.

For five years in a row, their corn and wheat crops failed. Farmers had no income, and couldn't pay their mortgages. And soon their financial troubles were matched by the horror of their surroundings.

THE SOIL BLEW AWAY

With no rainfall, the soil in the area became loose, dry, and dusty. The region's native wild grasses, which had served to hold the soil together, had been replaced long ago by crops, which now dried up and blew away.

Soon, heavy winds began to howl, picking up

from *Scholastic Scope*, V46, Issue 14, March 23, 1998, p. 15-16; photos from *Children of the Dust Bowl* by Jerry Stanley

the dust and soil. When the winds reached 50 or 60 miles an hour, they picked up the topsoil right off the ground. The flying dust buried roads. It flew through the walls and windows of flimsy farmhouses. It killed cattle, and ruined the engines of vehicles. Old people and children caught outside were suffocated. Thousands of others died slowly of "dust pneumonia."

The dust storms were the last straw for many area farmers. They had already suffered through five years with little or no income because of the drought. Now, banks and mortgage companies took their farms, sending tractors to knock their houses down and run them off the land. The farmers, with no other choice, packed up their families and meager belongings and headed west.

More than 1 million people migrated west from the Plains states during that time. Poor, dirty, and hungry, they rumbled down Route 66, searching for work picking crops, digging roads — anything that would keep their families from starving.

TOUGH TIMES

But things were tough in the West, too. There were not enough jobs for all the new arrivals. Few could afford housing. Most of the migrant families camped or "squatted" wherever they could.

Many native Californians resented the migrants, calling them "Okies," and spreading rumors that they were mentally retarded. They felt the migrants were

A migrant woman, recently widowed and the mother of six children, in an "Okieville" in 1936. This photograph, taken by Dorothea Lange, was widely published and, like John Steinbeck's novel The Grapes of Wrath, *drew the attention of the American public to the plight of the Okies in California.*

ruining local schools with overcrowding. Mobs of local men, armed with clubs and ax handles, raided the squatters' camps and tried to beat the migrants into leaving.

Eventually, as America came out of the Great Depression, things began to improve for the migrants in California. Within a few years, the rains returned to the Dust Bowl, and people began farming again. Over the decades since, there have been several other serious droughts in the Plains states. But the Dust Bowl of the 1930s will always be remembered as the worst of all.

An Okie mother and her two children in a squatter camp, or "Little Oklahoma," in 1936. Their broken-down car still has its Oklahoma license plate.

AN EYEWITNESS ACCOUNT

THE DUST I HAD LABORED IN ALL DAY BEGAN TO SHOW ITS EFFECTS ON MY SYSTEM. MY HEAD ACHED, MY STOMACH WAS UPSET, AND MY LUNGS WERE OPPRESSED AND FELT AS IF THEY MUST CONTAIN A TON A FINE DIRT.

—Lawrence Svobida
Kansas wheat farmer

How to Read Encyclopedia Articles

What Are Online Encyclopedias?

An online encyclopedia is much like a print encyclopedia. It contains non-fiction articles about many topics. Online/Internet encyclopedias offer the advantage of additional features such as Web links and clickable photos.

Why Are They Useful?

Online encyclopedias are great ways to find updated information on a topic quickly. The links provide further information as needed. They are easy to access and can be used at home, at school, in the library, or anywhere a computer exists. Therefore, they save a lot of time and expense.

✳

Direct Instruction

- Distribute the Online Encyclopedia Articles lesson, pages 100–101. Have students read it silently before discussing the model text together. Then, use the *color transparency* to guide students as they apply the Reading Tools.
- Use the Minilesson on page 99 to model the text feature.

Comprehension QuickCheck

After you have completed the lesson, you may use the following questions to check students' comprehension:

1. *What are online encyclopedias?* (collections of nonfiction articles on the Internet about a host of topics)
2. *Why are online encyclopedias helpful?* (You can find information quickly and easily.)
3. *What special features does this online encyclopedia article contain?* (links to other sites, a map, and illustrations of the person the article is about)
4. *If you wanted to learn about another famous person, which*

Materials

✳ Model Text, "Elizabeth I, Queen of England," p. 101

✳ Text Structure Transparency 10

✳ Bookmark, p. 160

would you choose—an online encyclopedia or a print encyclopedia? Why? (Answers will vary, but should be supported.)

Teaching the Text Feature

Introduce: Point out that online encyclopedias are very similar to print encyclopedias. They contain nonfiction articles about many topics. They also contain Web links for additional, related information. Tell students the following:

- Before you can research on the Internet, you must choose a *search engine.*

- Next, use the *search box.* This is an empty box, usually at the top of the search engine, in which you type the word or phrase that you want to research. Then click on the button labeled "search," "find," or "go" to begin your search.

- When the computer is finished searching, you will see pages of *search results,* or web sites that match your search.

- Read each *web site description* for each search result. Then choose a site that looks like it might be helpful.

- Once you're on the site, read the *title* to learn what the article is about.

- Scan for *subheadings* to identify main ideas in the text. They will also tell you about the topic of upcoming sections.

- Click on the *site search button* to be taken to other parts of the web site.

- Look for other text features such as *photographs, links, maps, special boxes,* and *underlined topics* that can bring up more information. Click on photographs and illustrations to enlarge them.

Model: Use the Think Aloud to model how to read an on-line source.

Guided Practice/Apply: Have students reread "Elizabeth I, Queen of England" on page 101 to learn about the famous ruler. Ask them to retell the information in their own words. You may also wish to ask the following:

1. *When did Elizabeth I live?* (from 1533 to 1603)

2. *What can you learn about her from the illustrations provided?* (You learn what she looked like and where she lived and reigned.)

3. *Why was Elizabeth's reign so famous?* (Answers may vary, but should include that England prospered during her reign.)

4. *What did Elizabeth's nickname "Good Queen Bess" tell about her?* (She was very well-loved by her people.)

5. *Where else could you find information about Elizabeth I?* (other encyclopedias, biographies, online articles, and so on)

The title tells me that this online encyclopedia entry is about Queen Elizabeth I of England. I see that the article about her is divided into sections according to important aspects of her life and rule. I also see the names of people associated with her that I can click on for further information. In addition, I see a map, photo, and drawing. These can be clicked on to enlarge them, and they provide even more information about this powerful and fascinating ruler.

Online Encyclopedia Articles

Suppose you wanted to learn more about a famous person from long ago. When did the person live? Why is the person famous? What interesting facts about the person should you know? You can use an online encyclopedia on the Internet to find this and other information about the person. Like a regular print encyclopedia, an online encyclopedia contains nonfiction articles about many topics. Internet encyclopedias also have extra features like Web links.

Reading Tools

In this lesson, you will be reading an online encyclopedia article. Use the Reading Tools below to help you find and read an online encyclopedia entry.

- Before you can research on the Internet, you must choose a search engine. There are many **search engines** to choose from, and your teacher may have a preference.

- Next, use the **search box**. This is an empty box, usually at the top of the search engine, in which you type the word or phrase that you want to research. Then click on the button labeled "search," "find," or "go" to begin your search.

- When the computer is finished searching, you will see pages of **search results**, or Web sites that match your search.

- Read each **Web site description** for each search result. Then choose a site that looks like it might be helpful.

- Once you're on the site, read the **title** to learn what the article is about.

- Scan for **subheadings** to identify main ideas in the text. They will also tell you about the topic of upcoming sections.

- Click on the **site search button** to be taken to other parts of the Web site.

- Look for other text features such as **photographs, links, maps, special boxes,** and **underlined topics** that can bring up more information. Click on photographs and illustrations to enlarge them.

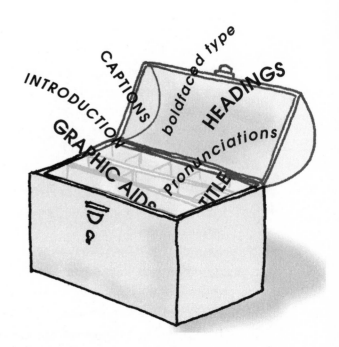

Remember to use these Reading Tools when you read encyclopedia articles.

Grolier Multimedia Encyclopedia

Browse a Category:

Geography

History: World

History: United States

Society and Government

Social Sciences

Language and Literature

Religion, Philosophy, Mythology

Performing Arts

Visual Arts

Life Sciences

Physical Science and Math

Technology

Sports, Games, Recreation

Features:

Brain Jam

News

Research Starters

Timelines

Advanced Search

About

Help

Receive e-mail updates

Elizabeth I, Queen of England

Print/Email · Periodicals · Web Links

Table of Contents

Elizabeth I, queen of England from 1558 to 1603, is famous for the glamour of her court and the success of her policies.

She was born on September 7, 1533, the daughter of Henry VIII and his second wife, Anne Boleyn. Henry, who had just had his marriage to Catherine of Aragon annulled and married Anne in the hope of begetting a male heir, was initially disappointed at Elizabeth's birth. He soon convinced himself, however, that Anne would eventually produce a son. When she failed to do so, she was executed in 1536. Elizabeth thus grew up without a mother's care, although Henry's last wife, Catherine Parr, was for a time an affectionate stepmother.

During the reign of her half brother, Edward VI, Elizabeth was involved in an episode with Thomas Seymour, whose brother was the Protector, Edward Seymour, duke of Somerset. For this and for a suspected attempt to gain improper influence over Edward VI, Thomas was executed (1549). While her half sister Mary I was queen (1553-58), Elizabeth lived quietly, awaiting her opportunity to succeed.

Religious Settlement and Foreign Affairs

Her reign began on Nov. 17, 1558, when Mary died. Elizabeth immediately named Sir William Cecil (later Lord Burghley) her chief minister, and with his help she concluded the famous Elizabethan Settlement for the Church of England (see England, Church of). Religion in England has been unsettled since Henry VIII's break with the pope in 1533. Moderate Protestantism had been practiced under Henry, and more radical Protestant programs were implemented under Edward VI; but Mary had restored the Roman Catholic faith and papal jurisdiction to England. Elizabeth herself was a moderate Protestant. Her settlement again excluded papal authority, and it brought back the Book of Common Prayer. Descendants of Henry VIII, the Tudor line was extinguished upon her death. Throughout her reign Elizabeth refused to designate a successor, but it is clear that she expected King James VI of Scotland to follow her. When Elizabeth died on Mar. 24, 1603, James, the son of Mary, Queen of Scots, but a Protestant, succeeded without incident as James I of England.

Stanford E. Lehmberg

Bibliography: Doran, Susan, *Monarchy and Matrimony: A Study of Elizabeth I's Courtships* (1996); Erickson, Carolly, *The First Elizabeth* (1984); Frye, Susan, *Elizabeth I* (1993); Haigh, Christopher, *Elizabeth I*, 2d ed. (1998); Hibbert, Christopher, *The Virgin Queen* (1991); MacCaffrey, Wallace T., *Elizabeth I: War and Politics, 1588–1603* (1992); Marcus, Leah, et al., eds., *Elizabeth I: Collected Works* (2000) Ridley, Jasper, *Elizabeth I* (1988); Strong, Roy, *The Cult of Elizabeth* (1977; repr. 1986); Weir, Alison, *The Life of Elizabeth I* (1998).

Reading "Hatshepsut: Woman Pharaoh"

Build Background

Students will be reading an encyclopedia article about Hatshepsut, the famous female ruler of Ancient Egypt. Create a blank Smart Chart and distribute copies or create one on butcher paper. Use the routine on page 24. Through your questioning, guide the discussion to identify students' knowledge and/or misconceptions about Ancient Egypt and its rulers.

Share with students the following information prior to reading:

- Hatshepsut was one of the few women to rule Egypt as a pharaoh—a term generally used to refer to a male ruler.
- She lived in Ancient Egypt around 1482 B.C.
- Her rule is remembered for its building programs, such as several great monuments.

Materials

✱ Model Text, "Hatshepsut: Woman Pharaoh," pp. 106–107

✱ Graphic Organizer, p. 105

Knowledge Rating Chart

	Can Define	Know Some Information About	Don't Know
pharaoh			
widow			
empire			
royal			
monument			
obelisk			

Preteach Vocabulary

Preteach the following words from "Hatshepsut: Woman Pharaoh" using the Vocabulary Routine on page 29. Or you may wish to use the Knowledge Rating Chart shown at left. After each student rates his or her knowledge of the words, follow up with a discussion of which words are the easiest, most difficult, most unfamiliar to the greatest number of students. Encourage students to share what they know about the words. The discussion will also give you an idea of how much knowledge students bring to the concepts they will be reading about.

Define each word and provide an example sentence. Be sure to point out unusual pronunciations, related words, and other aspects of the word.

- **pharaoh:** the title of kings of ancient Egypt. *King Tut was a young pharaoh in ancient Egypt.*

- **widow:** a woman whose husband has died and who has not married again. *The widow lived alone in her house for many years after her husband's death.*

- **empire:** a group of countries that have the same ruler. *Many countries belonged to the great Roman Empire.*

- **royal:** having to do with or belonging to a king, queen, or member of his/her family. *The princess looked beautiful at her royal wedding.*

- **monument:** a statue or building that is built to remind people of a specific person or event. *Our town had a stone monument made to honor those who fought in World War II.*

- **obelisk:** a tall, four-sided piece of stone with a pyramid top. *The giant Egyptian obelisk had hieroglyphics written all over it.*

Read the Selection

- Distribute copies of "Hatshepsut: Woman Pharaoh," pages 106–107. Have students preview the selection using the Preview Routine on page 41. Then, guide students as they apply the strategies they have learned for navigating text. Remind students to use the Reading Tools to read the article provided.

- Before the second reading, use the Minilesson below to teach students about the selection's text structure: sequence.

Minilesson

Teaching the Text Structure: Sequence

Introduce: Discuss the importance of identifying how text is structured. It alerts readers to how the text was written and can help them organize their thinking as they read. Tell students that an encyclopedia article about a person often includes details in the order in which they happened throughout the person's life.

Model: You may wish to use the Think Aloud as you model how to determine the text structure of "Hatshepsut: Woman Pharaoh."

Guided Practice/Apply: As students reread the selection, have them complete the graphic organizer for sequence, page 105. Then have students work in pairs to retell the information in their own words.

Think Aloud

Writers organize their writing in a way that helps us understand it.

I see that the article "Hatshepsut: Woman Pharaoh" is a biographical entry. Biographies are usually written in time-order, beginning with the person's birth, continuing through his/her major life accomplishments, then ending with his/her death. I see the date 1500 B.C. That tells me an important date in Hatshepsut's life.

I also see time-order key words and phrases such as around, soon, never before, within a few years, thus, eventually, *and* after twenty years. *This tells me that the article is written in time-order sequence.*

Comprehension QuickCheck

After you have completed the lesson, you may use the following questions to check students' comprehension:

1. *What does Hatshepsut's name mean?* ("most noble of noble women")
2. *What is Deir el Bahri?* (Hatshepsut's largest and most beautiful temple—and tomb. It is the greatest monument to a woman to survive the ancient world.)
3. *Why is Hatshepsut remembered today?* (She was a powerful, female ruler of Egypt and left behind some very important monuments.)
4. *How did the photographs add to your understanding of Hatshepsut?* (Answers will vary.)
5. *What else would you like to learn about ancient Egypt or Hatshepsut? How would you find this information?* (Answers will vary.)

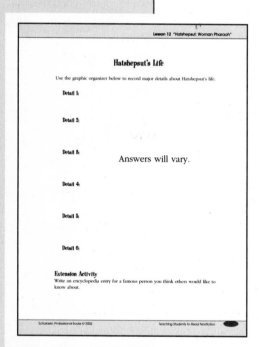

Independent Practice: Writing

Have students write a summary of the information they've just read. Suggest that they use the graphic organizer they completed while reading to help them create their summaries. Have them include the following:

- when Hatshepsut lived and reigned,
- why Hatshepsut is remembered today.

Web Links

www.archaeology.org	Archaeology Magazine
www.castles.org	Castles of the World
www.virtual-egypt.com	Virtual-Egypt.com
www.emulateme.com	Foreign Country Facts
encarta.msn.com	Encarta (historical topics)
www.historychannel.com	The History Channel

Hatshepsut's Life

Use the graphic organizer below to record major details about Hatshepsut's life.

Detail 1:

Detail 2:

Detail 3:

Detail 4:

Detail 5:

Detail 6:

Extension Activity

Write an encyclopedia entry for a famous person you think others would like to know about.

HATSHEPSUT:

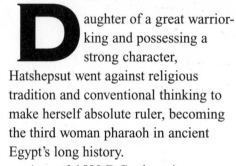

Daughter of a great warrior-king and possessing a strong character, Hatshepsut went against religious tradition and conventional thinking to make herself absolute ruler, becoming the third woman pharaoh in ancient Egypt's long history.

Around 1500 B.C., the princess, whose name means "most noble of noble women," entered her teens as the only child of King Thutmose and Great Royal Wife Ahmose. ("Great Royal Wife" was the title the ancient Egyptians gave to the pharaoh's spouse.) Because only men were supposed to rule, Hatshepsut was forced to marry her half-brother, also named Thutmose.

HATSHEPSUT BECOMES QUEEN

Hatshepsut became a widow at a rather young age. Not only did she have a daughter and a stepson to raise, but she also had an empire to rule. Her father had led Egypt's armies far into Asia, to the northern Euphrates River in what is now Syria. Egypt also held the gold-rich lands of Nubia and the Sudan, south of Egypt. Never before had such a huge territory, almost the entire known world, been within a pharaoh's powerful grasp. Egypt itself had flourished for fifteen hundred years of recorded history. It was a wealthy land, rich in natural resources and plentiful harvests.

As Thutmose III was still an infant when his father died, Hatshepsut was the only fully royal adult who could lead the government in his name. The queen soon found that she enjoyed the challenge and decided not to remarry. Within a few years, she came to feel that, along with all the responsibilities of governing, she deserved the titles and recognition that accompanied kingship. Thus, she proclaimed herself the legitimate king and planned for her daughter to succeed her to the throne.

RESTORING EGYPT

Secure borders and great wealth allowed Hatshepsut to pay attention to internal Egypt, and she set about restoring old temples and building new ones throughout the Nile valley. The largest and most beautiful was her funerary temple, now known as Deir el Bahri, the greatest monument to a woman to survive from the ancient world. This temple, built on three levels, had wall scenes depicting the shipping and erecting of the four gigantic obelisks (120 feet high and 320 tons each) brought to the temple at Karnak from the southern quarries at Aswan. Hatshepsut also sent trading expeditions to Punt, a distant land on the southwest coast of the Red Sea, which supplied Egypt with frankincense, rare African woods, and ivory.

Because it was so unusual for a woman to rule alone, Hatshepsut felt the need to proclaim her divinity on obelisks and the walls of her temples. A king of Egypt was regarded as the son of Amun-Re, the Egyptian king of the gods, so Hatshepsut called herself "Daughter of the God."

Hatshepsut also stressed the support her father had given her when he was alive, claiming that he would have

Adapted from "Hatshepsut: Woman Pharaoh," *Calliope*, Vol. 2, No. 2, Nov./Dec. 1991

WOMAN PHARAOH

wanted her to succeed him. She created a memorial chapel to him in her funerary temple, reburied him in her own tomb, often ignoring his grandson, who was kept in the background as he grew up.

A CAPABLE LEADER

Some of her father's former officials served her loyally, but Hatshepsut also had new advisors, whom she rewarded generously. Principal among these was Chief Steward Senmut, who tutored her daughter and oversaw all royal construction. Senmut may well have been the architect of the beautiful Deir el Bahri. On its walls, Hatshepsut is shown crushing her enemies beneath her feet. Indeed, it seems likely that she did not shy away from the battlefield. Two soldiers left records of following her into battle and witnessing her capture of Nubian chieftains. Perhaps the southern territories believed that having a woman on the throne would give them an opportunity to break away from Egypt's control, but they were mistaken. Hatshepsut was a capable leader in every sense.

Unfortunately, Hatshepsut's power could not ensure that all her dreams would come true. Her daughter died before her, and Thutmose III

eventually became king, as his father had wished. While Hatshepsut was still alive, she entrusted him with the leadership of the army, and he turned out to be the most successful military leader Egypt has ever known, ensuring that the great Egyptian Empire would continue for almost two more centuries to dominate the known world.

When Hatshepsut died after twenty years on the throne, she was buried in the Valley of the Kings along with other pharaohs of her dynasty. Twenty years later, Thutmose III began to destroy Hatshepsut's monuments in an effort to eliminate all traces of her reign. But enough of her records survive to show that she was one of the greatest women in the history of the world.

The Egyptians used obelisks as sacred symbols. These two graced the 250-acre religious complex at Karnak along the Nile River. Hatshepsut raised the one on the right, and her father raised the one on the left.

Hatshepsut (opposite) commissioned her architects to construct a magnificent temple (below) to house her mummy at the base of the cliffs at Deir el Bahri.

How to Read Online Sources

What Are Online News Articles?

An online news article is an article about a current event that is found on the Internet. To find an online article you need to use a search engine. Through a search engine you can enter a keyword or subject and the search engine will direct you to links containing related information. Some search engines also have pre-designated areas to search. These areas contain Web pages and Web site listings that the managers of the search engine have collected. Once you get to a Web page or site, follow the directions provided to navigate it.

Why Are They Useful?

Online news articles present up-to-date information that anyone can access quickly and for free. Using a simple search engine, a reader can find all the articles written on a particular topic, selecting those most appropriate for his or her reading needs. It is also easy to find a wide range of articles on any given topic faster than searching in a library.

——————————— ✳ ———————————

Materials

✳ Model Text, "The Oldest Dinosaurs?" p. 111

✳ Text Structure Transparency 11

✳ Bookmark, p. 160

Direct Instruction

- Distribute the Online News Article lesson, pages 110–111. Have students read it silently before discussing the model text together. Then, use the *color transparency* to guide students as they apply the Reading Tools.

- Use the Minilesson on page 109 to teach the text feature.

Comprehension QuickCheck

After you have completed the lesson, you may use the following questions to check students' comprehension:

1. *What are online news articles?* (Information about current events found on the Internet.)

2. *Why are online news articles helpful?* (You can find up-to-date information without leaving your seat.)

3. *What do these online news articles contain?* (facts, photos, links to other sites, etc.)

4. *If you wanted to find out about today's sports events, would an online news article be the best source? Why or why not?* (Answers will vary, but should be supported.)

5. *If you had to tell a classmate about online news articles, what would you say?* (Answers should reflect a clear understanding of online sources.)

Minilesson

Teaching the Text Feature

Introduce: Point out that online news articles contain information about current events and are found on the Internet. Tell students they should do the following to read an online news article:

- Read the *title*. It tells you what the article is about.

- Look for a *date*. It tells you when the article was written. You can decide if the news is up-to-date.

- Click on the *illustration* to make it larger and then read the *caption*.

- Click on the *underlined words* in the article. More information about the word or about the topic will pop up on your screen. You might also see an encyclopedia article about related topics.

- Look for *buttons*. You can click on these buttons or words to get more information. Sometimes links to a dictionary are provided.

Model: Use the Think Aloud to model how to read an online source.

Guided Practice/Apply: Have students read "The Oldest Dinosaurs?" on page 111 to learn about a dinosaur discovery. Ask them to retell the information in their own words. You may also wish to ask the following:

1. *Where did the scientists find the dinosaur fossils?* (in Madagascar, off the coast of Africa)

2. *Why was this find so special?* (The fossils may be the oldest ever found.)

3. *What did the dinosaur look like?* (It was about the size of a kangaroo—four to eight feet long. It had a small head and a long neck.)

4. *Is it possible that older dinosaur bones have been found? Why or why not?* (It is possible, since the article was written in 1999.)

5. *How would you find more information about dinosaur fossils?* (Answers will vary, but should include clicking on the Web links provided and/or using a search engine.)

Think Aloud

As I read the online news article, I discover that I have a lot of information at my fingertips. I can click on the photo to enlarge it, and I can click on underlined words to find their meanings. I can also click on the dictionary/thesaurus button to look up words and click on encyclopedia topics to get more information about dinosaurs and fossils. It's like having five or six articles in one.

Online News Articles

The Internet has opened up the world. Just turn on your computer and dial up and you can read an article about sports, find where movies are playing in your area, or do research for school. Your parents can even buy a car on the Internet! One of the most common types of writing found on the Internet is a news article.

Online news articles are popular because they offer up-to-date, minute-by-minute information. On the Internet, it is also easy to find articles from days, weeks, or even years past. In addition to the facts in the articles, these news reports often contain special features. With the click of your mouse you may be able to make a photograph larger, find more information about the topic, or use an online dictionary.

Reading Tools

In this lesson, you will be reading an online article. Use the Reading Tools below to help you read this type of article.

- Read the **title**. It tells you what the article is about.

- Look for a **date**. It tells you when the article was written. You can decide if the news is up-to-date.

- Click on the **illustration** to make it larger and then read the **caption**.

- Click on the **underlined words** in the article. More information about the word or about the topic will pop up on your screen. You can also see an encyclopedia article about related topics.

- Look for **buttons**. You can click on these buttons or words to get more information. This article has links to a dictionary and an interesting fact.

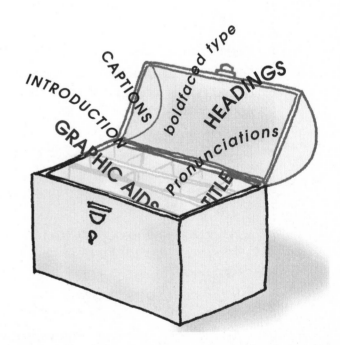

Remember to use these Reading Tools when you read online sources.

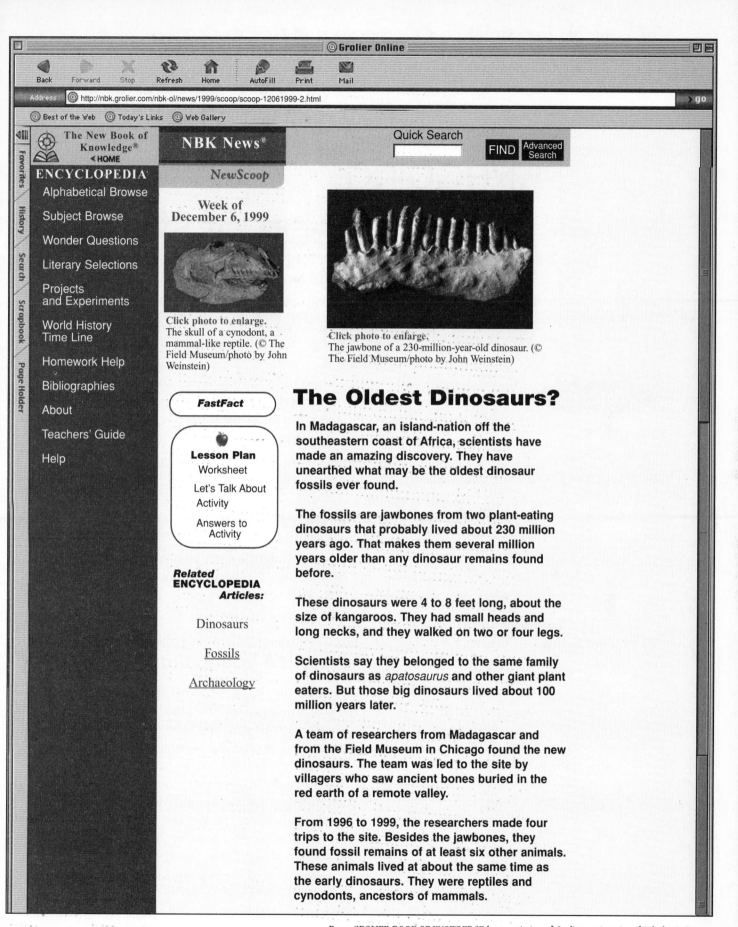

The Oldest Dinosaurs?

In Madagascar, an island-nation off the southeastern coast of Africa, scientists have made an amazing discovery. They have unearthed what may be the oldest dinosaur fossils ever found.

The fossils are jawbones from two plant-eating dinosaurs that probably lived about 230 million years ago. That makes them several million years older than any dinosaur remains found before.

These dinosaurs were 4 to 8 feet long, about the size of kangaroos. They had small heads and long necks, and they walked on two or four legs.

Scientists say they belonged to the same family of dinosaurs as *apatosaurus* and other giant plant eaters. But those big dinosaurs lived about 100 million years later.

A team of researchers from Madagascar and from the Field Museum in Chicago found the new dinosaurs. The team was led to the site by villagers who saw ancient bones buried in the red earth of a remote valley.

From 1996 to 1999, the researchers made four trips to the site. Besides the jawbones, they found fossil remains of at least six other animals. These animals lived at about the same time as the early dinosaurs. They were reptiles and cynodonts, ancestors of mammals.

The New Book of Knowledge®
◄ HOME

NBK News®

NewScoop

Week of December 6, 1999

Click photo to enlarge. The skull of a cynodont, a mammal-like reptile. (© The Field Museum/photo by John Weinstein)

Click photo to enlarge. The jawbone of a 230-million-year-old dinosaur. (© The Field Museum/photo by John Weinstein)

Quick Search

FIND | Advanced Search

ENCYCLOPEDIA

Alphabetical Browse

Subject Browse

Wonder Questions

Literary Selections

Projects and Experiments

World History Time Line

Homework Help

Bibliographies

About

Teachers' Guide

Help

FastFact

Lesson Plan
Worksheet
Let's Talk About Activity
Answers to Activity

Related
ENCYCLOPEDIA
Articles:

Dinosaurs

Fossils

Archaeology

Favorites | History | Search | Scrapbook | Page Holder

Back | Forward | Stop | Refresh | Home | AutoFill | Print | Mail

Address | @ http://nbk.grolier.com/nbk-ol/news/1999/scoop/scoop-12061999-2.html | ▸ go

@ Best of the Web | @ Today's Links | @ Web Gallery

@ Grolier Online

Reading "Willo's Heart of Stone"

Build Background

Students will be reading about another important dinosaur fossil discovery. Create a blank Smart Chart and distribute copies or create one on butcher paper. Use the routine on page 24. Through your questioning, guide the discussion to identify students' knowledge and/or misconceptions about dinosaurs.

Share with students the following information prior to reading:

- Dinosaurs lived from about 230 to 65 million years ago.

- Scientists believe that the earth grew colder and dinosaurs grew smaller. Smaller animals can be more active and have a higher body temperature.

- Around 65 million years ago, dinosaurs became extinct. One theory says that an asteroid 4–9 miles wide hit the earth. The dust caused by the impact could have blocked out sunlight for months, or even years. The loss of sunlight could have led to the death of plants and then the animals that depended on them for food.

Preteach Vocabulary

Preteach the following words from "Willo's Heart of Stone" using the Vocabulary Routine on page 29. Or you may wish to use the Knowledge Rating Chart shown at left. After each student rates his or her knowledge of the words, follow up with a discussion of which words are the easiest, most difficult, most unfamiliar to the greatest number of students. Encourage students to share what they know about the words. The discussion will also give you an idea of how much knowledge students bring to the concepts they will be reading about.

Materials

✳ Model Text, "Willo's Heart of Stone," pp. 116–117

✳ Graphic Organizer, p. 115

Knowledge Rating Chart

	Can Define	Know Some Information About	Don't Know
fossilized			
modern			
prehistoric			
underbrush			
computerized			

Define each word. Be sure to point out unusual pronunciations, compound words, related words, and other aspects of the word.

- **fossilized:** containing the remains or traces of an animal or a plant from millions of years ago. Focus on related words—*fossil, fossilize, fossil fuel.*

- **modern:** up-to-date, having to do with the present or the recent past. Focus on antonyms—*ancient, prehistoric.*

- **prehistoric:** belonging to a time before history was recorded in written form. Focus on the prefix *pre-*, meaning "before" (*pregame, preheat, premix, preorder, presale, preseason, prewash, prework*).

- **underbrush:** bushes, shrubs, and other plants that grow beneath the large trees in a forest. Focus on the prefix *under-*, meaning "below" (*underage, underbake, undercharge, underclothes, undercook, undercover, underground, undershirt*).

- **computerized:** controlled, processed, or stored by means of a computer. Focus on related words—*computer, computing, compute, computerize*—and the part of speech of each.

Read the Selection

- Distribute copies of "Willo's Heart of Stone," pages 116–117. Have students preview the selection using the Preview Routine on page 41. Then, guide students as they apply the strategies they have learned for navigating text. Remind students to use the Reading Tools to read the article provided.

- Before the second reading, use the Minilesson below to teach students about the selection's text structure: compare and contrast.

Minilesson

Teaching the Text Feature: Compare and Contrast

Introduce: Discuss the importance of identifying how text is structured. It alerts readers to how the text was written and can help them organize their thinking as they read. Tell students that this article tells how warm- and cold-blooded animals are alike and different, as well as comparing and contrasting Willo's heart to each type of animal.

Model: You may wish to use the Think Aloud to model how to determine the text structure of "Willo's Heart of Stone."

Guided Practice/Apply: As students reread the selection, have them complete the graphic organizer for compare and contrast, page 115. Then have students work in pairs to retell the information in their own words.

Think Aloud

Writers organize their writing in a way that helps us understand it.

The author of this article compares Willo's heart to hearts of warm- and cold-blooded animals. I read this sentence about dinosaurs, "Were they cold-blooded like reptiles, or warm-blooded like birds and mammals?" and notice the clue word like. *It tells me that Willo, a dinosaur, is being compared to warm-blooded animals.*

113

Comprehension QuickCheck

After you have completed the lesson, you may use the following questions to check students' comprehension:

1. *How big was Willo's heart?* (the size of a grapefruit)
2. *Why was Willo's find so special?* (No one had ever found a fossilized dinosaur heart before.)
3. *What kinds of animals does the article compare?* (warm- and cold-blooded animals)
4. *What special features do you see on the page?* (title, date, photograph, underlined words, hot buttons for more information)
5. *What other articles is the article linked to?* (articles on dinosaurs, birds, and fossils)

Possible Answers

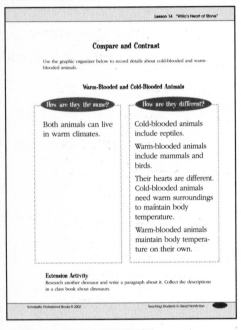

Independent Practice: Writing

Have students write a summary of the information they've just read. Suggest that they use the graphic organizer they completed while reading to help them create their summaries. Have them include the following:

- a description of Willo,
- why the Willo find was so important,
- the difference between warm- and cold-blooded animals.

Web Links

www.mos.org	Boston Museum of Science
www.amnh.org	American Museum of Natural History
www.fieldmuseum.org	The Field Museum of Natural History

Compare and Contrast

Use the graphic organizer below to record details about cold-blooded and warm-blooded animals.

Warm-Blooded and Cold-Blooded Animals

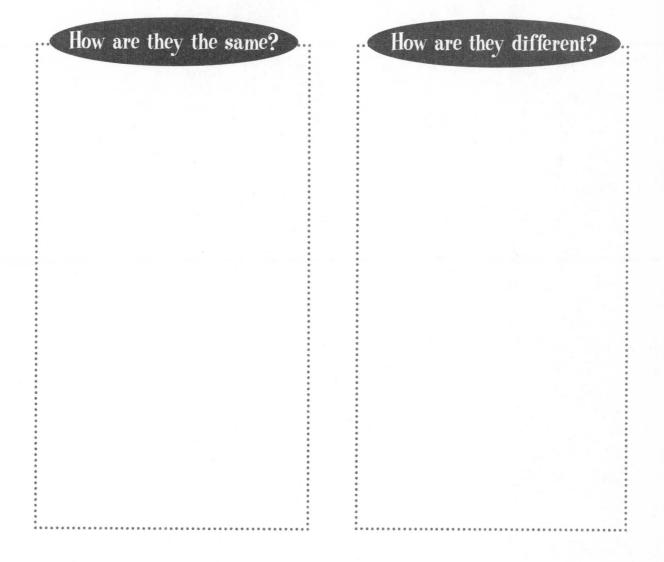

How are they the same?

How are they different?

Extension Activity

Research another dinosaur and write a paragraph about it. Collect the descriptions in a class book about dinosaurs.

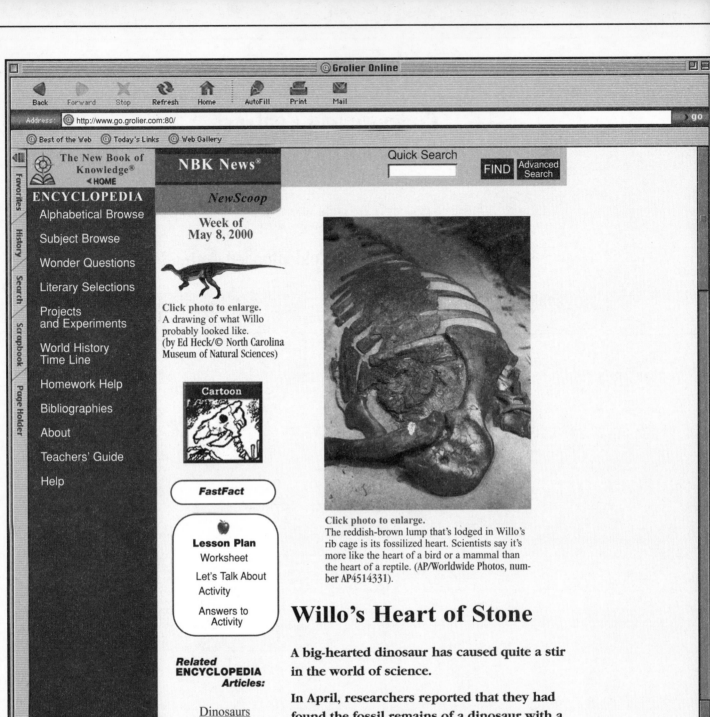

@ Grolier Online

Address: @ http://www.go.grolier.com:80/ 〉 go

@ Best of the Web   @ Today's Links   @ Web Gallery

The New Book of Knowledge®
◄ HOME

ENCYCLOPEDIA

Alphabetical Browse

Subject Browse

Wonder Questions

Literary Selections

Projects and Experiments

World History Time Line

Homework Help

Bibliographies

About

Teachers' Guide

Help

NBK News®

NewScoop

Week of May 8, 2000

Click photo to enlarge.
A drawing of what Willo probably looked like.
(by Ed Heck/© North Carolina Museum of Natural Sciences)

Cartoon

FastFact

Lesson Plan
Worksheet

Let's Talk About Activity

Answers to Activity

Related **ENCYCLOPEDIA** *Articles:*

Dinosaurs

Birds

Fossils

Quick Search

FIND   Advanced Search

Click photo to enlarge.
The reddish-brown lump that's lodged in Willo's rib cage is its fossilized heart. Scientists say it's more like the heart of a bird or a mammal than the heart of a reptile. (AP/Worldwide Photos, number AP4514331).

Willo's Heart of Stone

A big-hearted dinosaur has caused quite a stir in the world of science.

In April, researchers reported that they had found the fossil remains of a dinosaur with a heart the size of a grapefruit. That was amazing—no one had ever found a fossilized dinosaur heart before!

Even more surprising was what the scientists found when they examined the heart's structure. The dinosaur heart was more like the heart of a bird or a mammal than the heart of any modern reptile.

The discovery may help answer one unanswered question about dinosaurs: Were they cold-blooded, like modern reptiles, or warm-blooded, like birds and mammals? Cold-blooded animals need warm surroundings to maintain their body temperature. They slow down and become <u>sluggish</u> in the cold. Warm-blooded animals maintain their body temperature on their own. They stay active in the cold.

The "owner" of the newly discovered heart was a dinosaur that scientists have nicknamed Willo. Willo was a plant-eating dinosaur about 13 feet long. It weighed 665 pounds and was the size of a short-legged pony. This dinosaur lived around 66 million years ago.

Computerized X-ray scans show that the heart may have had four chambers, like the hearts of warm-blooded animals. Also like warm-blooded animals, this dinosaur seems to have had a single aorta. The aorta is the main artery that takes blood from the heart to the rest of the body.

Cold-blooded animals have simpler hearts, with three chambers, and two aortas. They pump blood less efficiently. That's one reason many reptiles are sluggish. With a four-chambered heart, Willo probably zipped around the underbrush of its prehistoric home. Speed would have helped it escape from giant meat-eating dinosaurs.

Willo may change our ideas about dinosaurs, scientists say. By the time this dinosaur lived, late in the Age of Reptiles, many dinosaurs may have been warm-blooded.

<u>Go to top of page.</u>

Grolier Online
◄Home

Dictionaries   Atlas

Search Grolier Online   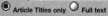 GO
⦿ Article Titles only ○ Full text

Scholastic Professional Books © 2002   *Teaching Students to Read Nonfiction*   **117**

How to Read Periodicals

What Are Periodicals?

Periodicals, such as newspapers and magazines, are nonfiction sources that are published at regular intervals—daily, weekly, monthly, or yearly. They often contain facts, quotes from persons knowledgeable on the topic, photographs, illustrations, charts, and other features.

Why Are They Useful?

Periodical articles tend to be rather short, specialized, and written at a high-interest level. They provide current information in an abbreviated form. Many contain firsthand accounts of events.

Direct Instruction

- Distribute the Periodicals lesson, pages 120–121. Have students read it silently before discussing the model text together. Then, display the *color transparency* and use it to guide students as they read and use the Reading Tools.

- Use the Minilesson on page 119 to teach the text feature.

Comprehension QuickCheck

After you have completed the lesson, you may use the following questions to check students' comprehension:

1. *What are periodicals?* (nonfiction sources, such as newspapers and magazines)

2. *Why are periodicals helpful?* (They provide current information in a very readable and interesting format.)

3. *What type of periodical is this article from?* (a magazine)

4. *What special features are included with this article? How do they help you understand the topic of the article?* (The photograph and chart provide additional information.)

Materials

✱ Model Text, "Danger: High Speed," p. 121

✱ Text Structure Transparency 12

✱ Bookmark, p. 160

Teaching the Text Feature

Introduce: Point out that periodicals are nonfiction sources, such as newspapers and magazines, that come out at regular intervals, such as every day or every month. To read a periodical article students should do the following:

- Look in the *table of contents* to find the pages related to their topic, such as the article title or subject area.

- *Preview* the text before they begin reading, as they would do with any nonfiction.

- Then *read the text* to learn about their topic. Attend to any special features, such as boldfaced words, charts, diagrams, maps, photographs, and so on.

- If the text includes *photographs or charts*, study them carefully. Photographs are a primary source that can provide details and additional information about a topic. Be sure to read the captions, as well. Charts provide a visual way to show a lot of information in a limited space.

- *Evaluate* the source. Look at the date on which it was written. Is the information up-to-date? Then look at the author's name. Is it written by an expert in that field of study?

Model: Use the Think Aloud to model how to use the text features in periodicals.

Guided Practice/Apply: Have students read "Danger: High Speed!" on page 121 to learn about speed and movement. Ask them to retell the information in their own words. You may also wish to ask the following:

1. *What sport does Venus Williams play?* (tennis)

2. *How fast is a baseball pitch?* (up to 124 miles per hour)

3. *Which object can move faster—a tennis ball or a soccer ball? Why?* (A tennis ball can move faster because it is smaller.)

4. *What causes a ball to slow down in the air?* (friction)

5. *Why do tennis officials want to increase the size of the tennis ball?* (Larger tennis balls would slow down the game and make it more interesting to watch.)

Think Aloud

The title tells me that this article has something to do with speed—maybe fast objects. Since the word "danger" is in the title, it must have something to do with objects moving at extremely fast speeds.

I see a photo of a famous tennis player, Venus Williams, beside the article. She is known for hitting the tennis ball very hard and very fast.

I also see a chart labeled "Fast Ball." I see the names of various sports moves, such as hitting a tennis ball or kicking a soccer ball.

So, I think this article will be about how fast objects, such as sports balls, move during sports activities.

Read About Science

Periodicals

Whether you're sitting on a train, relaxing on your front porch, or researching something for school, reading periodicals is a great way to find current and interesting articles on a wide range of topics. Periodicals, such as newspapers and magazines, are nonfiction sources that are published at regular intervals—daily, weekly, monthly, or yearly. They often contain facts, quotes from persons knowledgeable on the topic, photographs, illustrations, charts, and other features. Periodical articles tend to be rather short, specialized, and written at a high-interest level.

Reading Tools

In this lesson, you will be reading a magazine article. Use the Reading Tools below to help you read this type of periodical.

- Look in the **table of contents** to find the pages related to your topic, such as the article title or subject area.

- Before you begin reading, **preview** the text as you would do with any nonfiction.

- Then **read the text** to learn about your topic. Attend to any special features, such as boldfaced words, charts, diagrams, maps, photographs, and so on.

- If the text includes **photographs** or **charts**, study them carefully. Photographs are a primary source that can provide details and additional information about a topic. Be sure to read the captions, as well. Charts provide a visual way to show a lot of information in a limited space.

- **Evaluate** the source by looking at the date and author's name. Is the article current? Is it written by an expert?

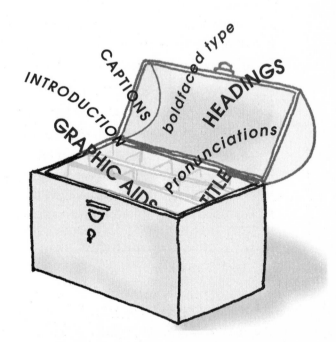

Remember to use these Reading Tools when you read periodicals.

Danger: High Speed!

Venus Williams serves up to 201 kph (125 mph).

Strong players using high-tech rackets are smacking tennis serves faster than ever. The world-record tennis serve is now 240 kph (149 mph); it's held by Greg Rusedski. Balls that fast are hard to hit back, say experts, making the game boring to watch. Some tennis officials want to slow the game.

How? They could change the size of the ball. As the ball flies, it passes through billions of air particles or **molecules**. The ball rubs against those molecules, causing **friction**, a force which slows the ball. A bigger ball would have more surface area and more friction, so it would travel more slowly. Tennis officials are experimenting with a ball that is 6 cm (just over 2 in) larger in diameter.

Graph questions: Which objects travel at the same speed? How much faster than a soccer shot is a hockey shot?

BOB FALCETTI/ICON SPORTS MEDIA

Fast Ball

	50 kph (31 mph)	100 kph (62 mph)	150 kph (93 mph)	200 kph (124 mph)	250 kph (155 mph)	300 kph (186 mph)	350 kph (217 mph)
Badminton smash							
Tennis serve							
Table tennis smash							
Ice hockey slapshot							
Baseball pitch							
Football pass							
Soccer shot							

from *Super Science* V13, Issue 1, September 2001, p. 4

Reading "Animals vs. Humans"

Build Background

Students will be reading a magazine article comparing the strength and speed of animals and Olympic athletes. Create a blank Smart Chart and distribute copies or create one on butcher paper. Use the routine on page 24. Through your questioning, guide the discussion to identify students' knowledge and/or misconceptions about animal adaptation.

Share with students the following information prior to reading:

- Animals have adapted to their environments in order to survive.

- Some animals, such as baboons, live in groups to protect each other. Other animals, such as birds, have modifications to their bodies (beaks) that enable them to collect food. This enables many types of animals to live in the same area and survive since each is eating different kinds of food. Still other animals, such as polar bears and camels, have adapted to the climates in which they live. Polar bears have a thick layer of fat; camels have thick foot pads designed for walking on hot sand and conserve water by recycling the moisture in their breath.

- Humans are the most adaptable animal. We have developed technology so that we can live anywhere.

Materials

✳ Model Text, "Animals vs. Humans,"
pp. 126–127

✳ Graphic Organizer,
p. 125

Word Connection

Write each pair of words on the chalkboard. Have students discuss how the words are related.

adaptation.....survive
species...........extinct

Preteach Vocabulary

Preteach the following words from "Animals vs. Humans" using the Vocabulary Routine on page 29. Or you may wish to use the Word Connection Chart shown in the sidebar. Encourage students to share what they know about each word pair. Then have them use the words in a sentence. The discussion will also give you an idea of how much knowledge students bring to the concepts they will be reading about.

Define each word and provide an example sentence. Be sure to point out unusual pronunciations, related words, and other aspects of the word.

- **adaptation:** a change that a living thing goes through so that it fits in better in its environment. *The shape of bird beaks is an example of an animal adaptation. For example, some beaks are long and pointy for picking up small insects.* Focus on related words: *adapt, adapter, adaptable, adapting, adapted.*

- **survive:** to stay alive through some dangerous event; to continue to live. *Did the man survive 100 days alone on that deserted island?* Focus on related words: *survival, survivor.*

- **species:** a group of related animals or plants. *The cheetah and the Siamese are two different species of cat.* Focus on pronunciation: *spee-sheez* or *spee-seez.*

- **extinct:** died out. *The dinosaur is now extinct. No dinosaurs live on Earth.* Focus on related words: *extinction, extinguish, exterminate.*

Read the Selection

- Distribute copies of "Animals vs. Humans," pages 126–127. Have students preview the selection using the Preview Routine on page 41. Then, guide students as they apply the strategies they have learned for navigating text. Remind students to use the Reading Tools to read the article provided.

- Before the second reading, use the Minilesson below to teach students about the selection's text structure: compare and contrast.

Minilesson

Teaching the Text Structure: Compare and Contrast

Introduce: Discuss the importance of identifying how text is structured. It alerts readers to how the text was written and can help them organize their thinking as they read. Tell students that this article tells how animals and Olympic athletes are alike in terms of physical ability.

Model: You may wish to use the Think Aloud as you model how to determine the text structure of "Animals vs. Humans."

Guided Practice/Apply: As students reread the selection, have them complete the graphic organizer for compare and contrast, page 125. Then have students work in pairs to retell the information in their own words.

Think Aloud

Writers organize their writing in a way that helps us understand it.

I see that the title says "Animals vs. Humans." That means that animals are being compared or "pitted against" humans in some way.

In the photos I see people running, and jumping. Beside each photo is an animal performing the same task.

Therefore, animals and humans are being compared in terms of their physical abilities.

Comprehension QuickCheck

After you have completed the lesson, you may use the following questions to check students' comprehension:

1. *Why do animals need to adapt?* (in order to survive their environments, live long lives, and have many babies)

2. *What happens to animals that don't adapt?* (They die young.)

3. *Why did the author choose Olympic athletes to compare to animals?* (because they run the fastest and jump the farthest of all humans)

4. *Where do kangaroos live?* (in open forests and grasslands)

5. *How do the photographs help you understand the topic?* (Answers will vary, but should be supported.)

Possible Answers

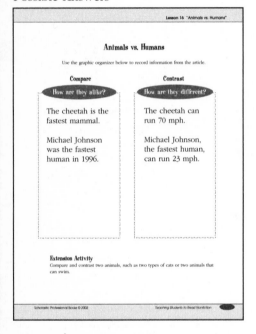

Independent Practice: Writing

Have students write a summary of the information they've just read. Suggest that they use the graphic organizer they completed while reading to help them create their summaries. Have them include the following:

- how animals have adapted to their environments,

- why adaptation is necessary.

Web Links

www.sandiegozoo.org   San Diego Zoo

animaldiversity.ummz.umich.edu/   University of Michigan
  index.html

Animals vs. Humans

Use the graphic organizer below to record information from the article.

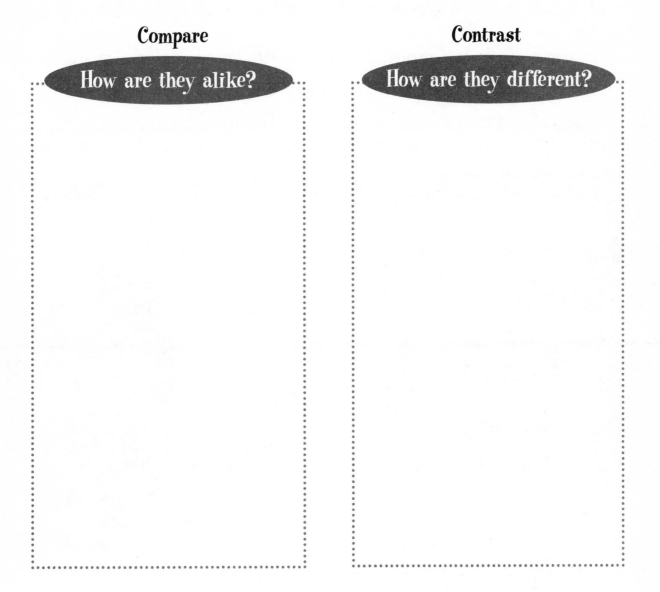

Compare

How are they alike?

Contrast

How are they different?

Extension Activity

Compare and contrast two animals, such as two types of cats or two animals that can swim.

Animals vs. Humans

In the Olympic Games, humans battle humans in a stadium. But in the SuperScience contest, Olympians compete against animals in the animals' environment. Who will win?

THE CHEETAH

Animals are masters of adaptation. They have to be to survive. In nature, the best adapters live long lives and have many babies. They pass their ability to jump, run, and survive to their offspring. Animals that don't adapt die young. Eventually, species can become extinct.

Look on these pages and you'll see amazing examples of adaptation. The human performances are world-class, too. But could the humans compete in the animals' environment? You decide. Fill in each blank with the winner's name.

MICHAEL JOHNSON

VS.

The event: Sprint

The environment: Grassy plains

The competitors: Cheetah vs. Michael Johnson of the U.S.A.

The finish line: The cheetah can run 113 kph (70 mph). In the 1996 Olympic Games, Johnson set a world record and captured the gold medal when he ran 200 m in 19.32 seconds. That's 37 kph (23 mph).

The winner is: _____

ASHIA HANSEN

THE KANGAROO

The event: Triple jump

The environment: Open forests and grasslands

The competitors: Red kangaroo vs. Ashia (Ash-E-uh) Hansen of Germany

The finish line: The kangaroo can bound 8 m (26 ft) in one hop. That would make a triple jump of 25 m (82 ft)! In the 1999 world Championships, Hansen jumped 15.02 m (49.28 ft).

The winner is: _____

VS.

THE OSTRICH

The event: Long-distance running

The environment: Sandy grasslands and deserts

The competitors: Ostrich vs. Gabriela Szabo (Gab-ree-EL-la ZA-bow) of Romania, a country in Europe

VS.

The finish line: Ostriches can run more than 48 kph (30 mph) for 30 minutes. They could run 5,000 m (3 miles in 6 minutes, 15 seconds). Szabo holds the world indoor record in the 5,000-m run. She ran this distance in just over 14 minutes, 30 seconds.

The winner is: _____

GABRIELA SZABO

from *Super Science*, V12, 2000-2001

How to Read Multi-Tiered Time Lines

What Are Multi-Tiered Time Lines?

A multi-tiered time line is a more sophisticated type of time line. Each tier, or part of the time line, shows events that occurred in different places at the same time. Multi-tiered time lines can also show different types of events that occurred in the same place.

Why Are They Useful?

Multi-tiered time lines can show related events or put events in historical perspective in a visually-simple way. For example, it is interesting to know what was happening in the rest of the world during the colonial period in the United States. Students may not realize the connections between the great events in the rest of the world and those in the United States. Often, these events affect each other in ways that are not easily recognized. Multi-tiered time lines are effective in providing a more global look at any time period.

─────────────────────── ✽ ───────────────────────

Direct Instruction

- Distribute the Multi-Tiered Time Line lesson, pages 130–131. Have students read it silently before discussing the model text together. Then, use the *color transparency* to guide students as they apply the Reading Tools.

- Use the Minilesson on page 129 to teach the text feature.

Comprehension QuickCheck

You may use the following questions to check students' comprehension:

1. *What are multi-tiered time lines?* (diagrams that show when events happened and that contain more than one layer of information)

2. *Why are multi-tiered time lines helpful?* (They provide information about a lot of events in many places in a small space.)

3. *What does this time line show?* (The historical events, inventions,

Materials

✽ Model Text, "The Amazing 1800s: U.S. History, Inventions, and Daily Life," p. 131

✽ Text Structure Transparency 13

✽ Bookmark, p. 160

and major daily life accomplishments in the United States throughout the 1800s.)

4. *If you wanted to create a multi-tiered time line about the past year, what categories of information would you include and why?* (Answers will vary, but should be supported.)

5. *If you had to tell a classmate about multi-tiered time lines, what would you say?* (Answers should reflect a clear understanding of multi-tiered time lines.)

Minilesson

Teaching the Text Feature

Introduce: Point out that time lines are a special type of graphic aid that shows a series of events and the dates on which they happened. A multi-tiered time line is a more sophisticated time line with multiple layers of information. To read multi-tiered time lines students should:

- First, read the *title* of the multi-tiered time line. It tells them what historical period the time line covers.

- Look at the titles of each *tier.* They tell readers in which part of the world the event took place. They can also tell sub-categories of events in the same place.

- Find the starting and ending *dates* for each series of events. Some time lines, like this one, are horizontal. You read those from left to right. Other time lines are vertical. Those are read from the top to the bottom of the page.

- Read the *labels* for each date. They describe each event.

Model: Use the Think Aloud to model how to read the time line.

Guided Practice/Apply: Have students read "The Amazing 1800s: U.S. History, Inventions, and Daily Life" on page 131 to learn about this historic time period. Ask them to retell the information in their own words. You may also wish to ask the following:

1. *What place and time period are covered in this time line?* (the United States during the 1800s)

2. *What important inventions that you use today emerged during the 1870s?* (telephone and lightbulb)

3. *When were blue jeans first created?* (1850)

4. *What also happened during the year in which the first coast-to-coast railroad was completed?* (Chewing gum was patented.)

5. *Which category of information is most interesting to you and why?* (Answers will vary, but should be supported.)

Think Aloud

The title tells me that this time line covers a specific time period in a specific place—the 1800s in the United States.

As I look down the left-hand side, I see three categories of information—U.S. History, Inventions, and Daily Life. These are the three groupings of information provided in the time line. It will be interesting to see, for example, what people were doing in their daily lives and what inventions were created during the Civil War in the mid-1800s. This time line will provide that information and more.

Multi-Tiered Time Lines

What happened? and When? are two common questions you might ask yourself when learning about a new topic or time period. For example, you might want to know what happened in the United States in the 1700s. To find out this information you could look at a time line. A time line is a special type of diagram. It shows a series of events and the years in which they happened. This information is always presented in chronological order. Time lines contain a lot of information in a limited space, making it easy to learn about a time period at a glance.

A multi-tiered time line is a more sophisticated type of time line. Each tier, or part of the time line, shows events that occurred in different places at the same time. For example, if you wanted to know what was happening in the United States and in Africa in the 1700s, a multi-tiered time line could show that. Multi-tiered time lines can also show different types of events that occurred in the same place, such as politics, science, and sports events in the United States in the 1980s.

Reading Tools

In this lesson, you will be reading a multi-tiered time line. Use the Reading Tools below to help you read it.

- First, read the **title** of the multi-tiered time line. It tells you what historical period the time line covers.

- Look at the titles of each **tier**. They tell you in which part of the world the event took place. They can also tell you subcategories of events in the same place.

- Find the starting and ending **dates** for each series of events. Some time lines, like this one, are horizontal. You read those from left to right. Other time lines are vertical. You read those from the top to the bottom of the page.

- Read the **labels** for each date. They describe each event.

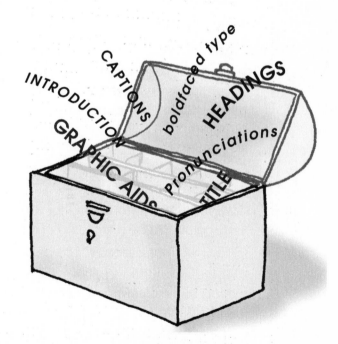

Remember to use these Reading Tools when you read multi-tiered time lines.

The Amazing 1800s: U.S. History, Inventions, and Daily Life

Timeline spanning 1800–1900.

U.S. History

1800	Washington, D.C., becomes U.S. capital.
1803	Louisiana Purchase from France doubles U.S. size.
1803	Lewis & Clark explore Louisiana & Northwest Territories.
1812-1814	War of 1812 fought between U.S. and Britain.
1819	U.S. acquires Florida from Spain.
1830	Indian Removal Act forces Native Americans west of Mississippi River.
1836	Texans defend the Alamo.
1838	Cherokee Nation forced west on "Trail of Tears."
1846	Mexican War gives U.S. Southwestern territories.
1846	Britain cedes Oregon Country to U.S.
1848	Gold discovered in California.
1860	Abraham Lincoln elected 16th president of the U.S.
1861	Civil War begins when Confederates fire on Fort Sumter.
1862	Lincoln proclaims abolition of slavery in U.S.
1869	Coast-to-coast railroad is finished in Utah.
1876	Custer defeated at Battle of Little Big Horn.
1889	Jane Addams founds Hull House in Chicago to help immigrants.
1898	U.S. defeats Spain in Spanish-American War.

Inventions

1800	The battery is invented by Count Volta.
1802	Steamboat is built by Robert Fulton.
1816	Stethoscope invented by René Laënnec.
1817	The Erie Canal is begun.
1836	Samuel Morse invents telegraph.
1839	Bicycle is invented by Kirkpatrick Macmillan.
1841	Stapler is developed.
1846	Elias Howe invents sewing machine.
1852	Elisha Otis invents first elevator with a safety break.
1874	Barbed wire introduced by Joseph Glidden.
1876	Alexander Graham Bell invents telephone.
1879	Thomas Edison makes incandescent lightbulb.
1887	Radio waves produced by Heinrich Hertz.
1893	Charles and Frank Duryea build first successful U.S. gasoline automobile.
1896	Gugielmo Marconi invents wireless radio.

Daily Life

1804	First book of children's poems is published.
1812	Army meat inspector, "Uncle Sam" Wilson, becomes U.S. symbol.
1814	Francis Scott Key writes "The Star-Spangled Banner."
1816	Niepce takes first photograph.
1820	Rip Van Winkle is written by Washington Irving.
1828	Webster's Dictionary is published.
1834	Louis Braille perfects a letter system for the blind.
1835	Hans Christian Anderson publishes Tales Told to Children.
1849	Safety pin is invented.
1850	Levi Strauss produces blue jeans.
1864	Red Cross is established.
1869	Chewing gum is patented.
1873	The zipper is invented by Whitcomb Judson.
1883	Four U.S. time zones are established.
1886	Dr. Penberton invents Coca-Cola.
1889	Roll film produced by George Eastman.
1892	The first basketball game is played.

"Historical Line" pages 893-894 from WRITE SOURCE 2000: A GUIDE TO WRITING, THINKING AND LEARNING. Text copyright (c) 1995 by Great Source Education Group, Inc. Reprinted by permission of Great Source Education Group, Inc. All rights reserved.

Reading "1763-1776: The Road to Revolution"

Build Background

Students will be reading a multi-tiered time line about the events that led to the Revolutionary War. Create a blank Smart Chart and distribute copies or create one on butcher paper. Use the routine on page 24. Through your questioning, guide the discussion to identify students' knowledge and/or misconceptions about the pre-Revolutionary time period in what is now the United States.

If necessary, share the following:

* In the 1760s, the United States was not yet a country. It consisted of thirteen colonies and was governed by Great Britain, also known as England. Great Britain was a world superpower.

* The ruler of Great Britain at this time was King George III.

* The colonists were upset that they could not govern themselves and that Great Britain imposed laws on them without allowing them to argue for or against them. That is, the colonists had no "political voice".

Preteach Vocabulary

Preteach the following words from "1763–1776: The Road to Revolution" using the Vocabulary Routine on page 29. Or you may wish to use the Knowledge Rating chart shown at left. After each student rates his or her knowledge of the words, follow up with a discussion of which words are the easiest, most difficult, most unfamiliar to the greatest number of students. Encourage students to share what they know about the

Materials

* Model Text, "1763–1776: The Road to Revolution," pp. 136–137
* Graphic Organizer, p. 135

Knowledge Rating Chart

	Can Define	Know Some Information About	Don't Know
colonies			
independence			
opposed			
rebel			
declare			

words. The discussion will also give you an idea of how much knowledge students bring to the concepts they will be reading about.

Define each word. Be sure to point out additional multiple meanings, related words including synonyms, multiple pronunciations, and other aspects of the word.

- **colonies:** lands that are settled by people from another country and controlled, or governed, by that country. Point out the related word: *colonists*

- **independence:** freedom. Point out the related word: *independent*.

- **opposed:** against. Point out the related words: *opposition, opposite*.

- **rebel:** to fight against something or someone. Point out the noun and verb form/pronunciations of the word.

- **declare:** to state. Point out the related word: *declaration* (i.e., Declaration of Independence).

Read the Selection

- Distribute copies of "1763–1776: The Road to Revolution," pages 136–137. Have students preview the selection using the Preview Routine on page 41. Then, guide students as they apply the strategies they have learned for navigating text. Remind students to use the Reading Tools to read the multi-tiered time line included in the article.

- Before the second reading, use the Minilesson below to teach students about the selection's text structure: sequence.

Think Aloud

Writers organize their writing in a way that helps us understand it. I see that the article "1763–1776: The Road to Revolution" presents information in a sequence.

Each paragraph contains dates beginning in 1763 and continuing until 1775. The attached time line is also an indicator that the sequence of events is important in this article.

Minilesson

Teaching the Text Structure: Sequence

Introduce: Discuss the importance of identifying how text is structured. It alerts readers to how the text was written and can help them organize their thinking as they read. Tell students that historical articles are often written in chronological, or time, order.

Model: You may wish to use the Think Aloud as you model how to determine the text structure of "1763–1776: The Road to Revolution."

Guided Practice/Apply: As students reread the selection, have them record the information that is in both the article and the time line on the graphic organizer, page 135. Then have students work in pairs to retell the information in their own words. What new information does the time line provide?

Comprehension QuickCheck

After you have completed the lesson, you may use the following questions to check students' comprehension:

1. *Why is the time period covered in the article and time line important?* (It details the events that led to the formation of the United States.)

2. *Who governed the United States in the 1760s?* (King George III of Great Britain)

3. *Who were the people living in the colonies that did not want independence? Why?* (The loyalists did not want to break ties with Great Britain.)

4. *How does the time line help you?* (Answers will vary.)

5. *How are the time line and article related?* (Answers should reflect a clear understanding of the contents of the time line.)

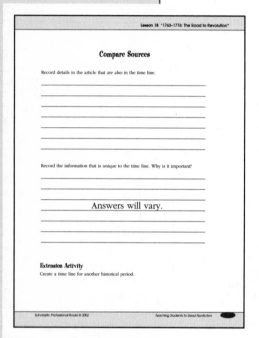

Independent Practice: Writing

Have students go to **www.earlyamerica.com**, find something else about the early years in what is now the United States, and in their own words write about it.

Web Links

www.whitehouse.gov	The White House
www.americaslibrary.gov	"America's Story" from the Library of Congress
www.nhmccd.edu/contracts/lrc/kc/decades.html	American Cultural History: The 20th Century
www.historychannel.com	The History Channel
www.earlyamerica.com	Early America

Compare Sources

Record details in the article that are also in the time line.

_____

_____

_____

_____

_____

Record the information that is unique to the time line. Why is it important?

_____

_____

_____

_____

Extension Activity

Create a time line for another historical period.

★ ★ 1763–1776 ★ ★
The Road to Revolution

Imagine that you lived in one of Britain's 13 colonies in 1775. If asked, you probably would say that you were a British subject, not an American. Yet, that year, events would begin to change your world. In April, American and British forces clashed in Massachusetts. A year later, the U.S. declared its independence.

Trouble had been brewing for more than 10 years. In 1763, Britain defeated France in the French and Indian War (see time line). Britain then tried to tighten control over its 13 American colonies and tax the colonies more heavily.

Colonists protested the taxes on paper, tea, and other items. "Why should

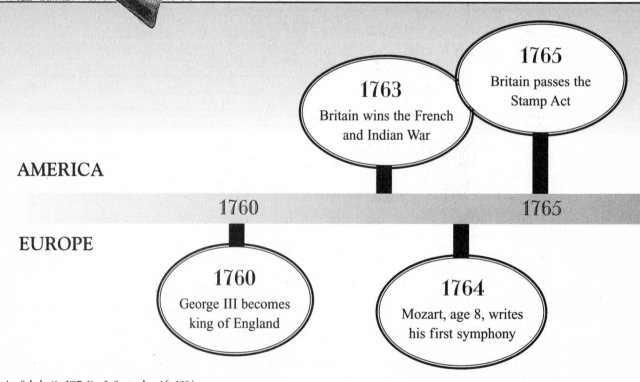

AMERICA

1763
Britain wins the French and Indian War

1765
Britain passes the Stamp Act

1760

1765

EUROPE

1760
George III becomes king of England

1764
Mozart, age 8, writes his first symphony

from *Junior Scholastic*, V97, No. 2, September 16, 1994

we pay British taxes when we have no say in passing them?" many asked.

People in Boston became so angry that one night in 1773, a group of them boarded a British ship and dumped its cargo of tea into the harbor (see the painting at right).

This made King George III furious. Britain's parliament (legislature) passed laws that put Massachusetts under military control. Americans called them the Intolerable Acts. This led to the first battles of the American Revolution, at Lexington and Concord in 1775.

Even then, not all Americans wanted to break their ties with Britain. Patriots wanted

The Boston Tea Party

independence; Loyalists were opposed to it.

Which side would you have taken if you lived in 1775? Remember, rebelling against Britain—the most powerful country in the world—was a huge gamble. No one knew how the American Revolution would turn out.

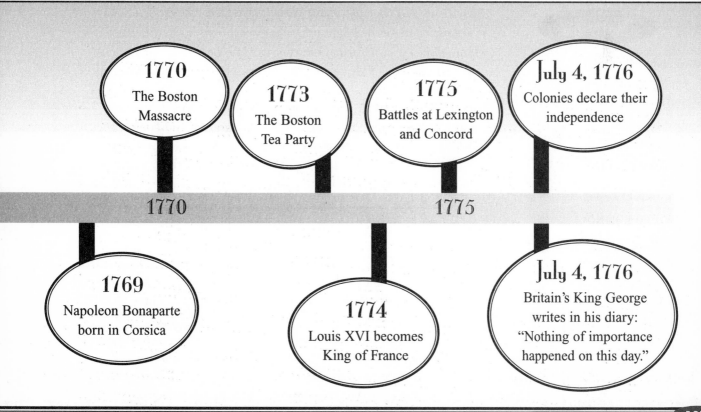

1770 The Boston Massacre

1773 The Boston Tea Party

1775 Battles at Lexington and Concord

July 4, 1776 Colonies declare their independence

1770   1775

1769 Napoleon Bonaparte born in Corsica

1774 Louis XVI becomes King of France

July 4, 1776 Britain's King George writes in his diary: "Nothing of importance happened on this day."

How to Read a Science Textbook

Multiple Features of Science Textbooks

Textbook reading can be very intimidating to some students for reasons that have been discussed in detail in Section 1 of this book. It is important to reassure students that they can learn to recognize the features in their textbooks that serve as aids in reading. These features are signposts will help students navigate their way through the complex-looking pages of a science textbook. Use examples from the students' science textbook as you discuss the following features:

- The information in the textbook is organized into various chapters. Each chapter is about a particular topic. The *chapter title* tells the reader what the topic is.
- Each chapter is divided into parts or sections. These parts have *headings* that tell the reader what the section is about.
- Reading the chapter title and the headings give the reader a good idea of the *important ideas* that will be covered.
- *Boldfaced words* highlight important vocabulary related to the topic.
- Sometimes a particular word that may be unfamiliar or difficult to pronounce is followed by its *pronunciation* written in brackets or parenthesis.
- *Graphic aids,* such as diagrams, graphs, and charts, illustrate particular information in the text. Some graphic aids provide additional information. Sometimes the reader has to stop reading the text, refer to a graphic aid, and then continue reading where he or she left off.

Direct Instruction

- Distribute the Science Textbook lesson, pages 140–141. Have students read it silently. Then, display the *color transparency* and use it to guide students as they read and use the Reading Tools.
- Use the Minilesson to teach the text feature. As students go back and forth from the text to the diagram, give them a "tip" for holding their place in the text: *To keep your place in the text, put a finger down at the spot where you stopped reading. Do this each time you stop reading to look at the diagram.*

Materials

✳ Model Text, "What Is Under Earth's Surface?," p. 141

✳ Text Structure Transparency 14

✳ Bookmark, p. 160

Minilesson

Teaching the Text Feature

Introduce: Remind students that a *diagram* is a labeled drawing that shows how something works or how the parts of something are arranged. The diagram on page 141 shows a cross-section of the earth. It illustrates the information given in the text. Point out the inset and explain that it is an enlargement of one section of the diagram. The inset allows you to see part of the diagram in detail.

Explain to students how to read a diagram:

- Study the diagram to see what it is showing. Figure out how each section is related to the whole.

- Read the labels for each part of the diagram.

- As you read the text, stop and go to the diagram. Find the part of the diagram that the text is discussing. Use the diagram to help you visualize the information in the text. Then go back and continue reading from where you left off.

- Continue to go back and forth between the text and the diagram until you finish reading.

- Be sure to read the caption, if there is one. It will give additional information.

- Make inferences based on the information in the diagram.

Model: Use the Think Aloud to model how to read a diagram.

Guided Practice/Apply: Have students read "What's Under Earth's Surface?" Ask them to explain:

- how the information in the diagram helps them understand the text.

- how they used each special feature to understand what they read.

Think Aloud

I can see that this diagram is a cross-section of the earth. It shows the layers inside the earth. I study the diagram and read the labels.

The inset shows the earth's crust. From looking at it, I realize that the crust is more than just the land we see. It's also found under the ocean.

As I read each paragraph in the text, I look at the diagram to see the information pictured. I start by finding the crust, then the mantle, and last the two parts of the core. When I study the diagram, I can make an inference about which layer is the thinnest and which is the thickest.

Comprehension QuickCheck

After you have completed the lesson, you may wish to ask the following:

1. *What are the layers of Earth?* (the crust, mantle, and core or outer core and inner core)

2. *Some science sources say that the earth is made up of three layers. Others say four layers. How do you explain this?* (If you count the core as one layer, there are 3 layers all together. If you count the outer core and inner core separately, there are 4.)

3. *Which layer is the thinnest?* (the crust) *Which is the thickest?* (the outer core and inner core combined)

4. *If a scientist tried to drill a hole through the crust to the mantle, where would he or she start drilling? Why?* (under the ocean because the crust is thinner than under land)

Read About Science

Science Textbook

A lot of the information you read in school comes from textbooks. You might have a textbook for each subject that you study, such as math, social studies, and science.

You have probably noticed that a textbook has more than just text in it. There are many features that help explain the information—features such as headings, diagrams, charts, and questions. Sometimes all this "stuff" on a page makes reading very difficult. Where do you start? What do you look at first? Actually, these features are there to help you. Once you know how to use them, you'll better understand and remember what you read.

Reading Tools

In this lesson, you will be reading a section of a science textbook. Use the tools below to help you read the science lesson.

- Read the **title** and **introduction**. They tell you what the lesson is about.

- Read the **headings**. They provide an outline of the most important ideas in the text.

- After your **preview**, say to yourself, "This lesson will be about…"

- As you read, try to remember the **boldfaced words**. They are important vocabulary terms that relate to the lesson.

- Use the **pronunciations** following words that may be unfamiliar or unusual.

- Study the **graphic aids**, such as any charts, diagrams, graphs, or tables. They will help you visualize the information in the text. They may also give you additional information.

- Answer the **questions** in the text to yourself. This will allow you to check your understanding.

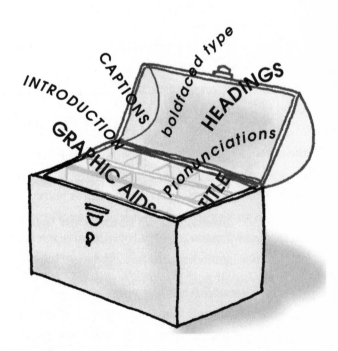

Remember to use these Reading Tools when you read science textbooks.

What Is Under Earth's Surface?

A journey to the center of Earth is only possible in movies or in your imagination. It's about 6,400 kilometers (4,000 miles) from the surface to the center, but just 5 kilometers (3 miles) down, the temperature is high enough to boil your blood. What does Earth look like once you really start to dig down?

Layers of the Earth

The hard outer crust is the coolest part of Earth. Almost three quarters of the crust is covered by water. The landforms you see on the surface, the continents, are parts of the crust that stick up above the ocean. Where is the crust thickest, under the oceans or under the continents?

The **mantle** is the next layer down. Between the mantle and the crust, melted rock called **magma** forms. The top of the mantle is hard and brittle, but just below is a deep layer of solid but puttylike rock. The deeper you go, the hotter it gets. No one has ever visited the mantle, but scientists think the temperature at the bottom is around 3,000° Celsius (SEL-see-us). That is 5,432° Fahrenheit (FA-ren-hite).

The **core** is the deepest layer. The outer part of the core is liquid, but the inner core, the very center of Earth, is so tightly packed that it's solid, even though the temperature may be as high as 6,000° C (10,832° F).

Inner core
6,000°C (10,832°F)

Outer core 4,000°C (7,232°F)

Mantle 3,000°C (5,432°F)

Crust 900°C (1,652°F)

Continental crust

Oceanic crust

▶ The crust of Earth is between 5 and 32 km (3 and 20 mi) thick. If Earth were an apple, its crust would be about as thick as the apple's skin.

Science Place, Vol. 5, 1995, Scholastic, Inc.

Reading "Journey Beneath the Earth"

Materials

✳ Model Text, "Journey Beneath the Earth," pp. 146–147

✳ Graphic Organizer, p. 145

Concept Circles

Draw the following concept circles on the chalkboard, one at a time. Have students read the two words in the circle and then add a related vocabulary word to complete the circle. Ask students to explain the basis for their choice.

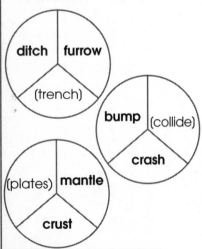

Build Background

Students will read a section of a science textbook about Earth's plates and a giant ring of more than 300 volcanoes. In order to comprehend the text, students need to know what lies below the surface of the earth. Create a blank Smart Chart and distribute copies or create one on butcher paper. Use the routine on page 24. Through your questioning, guide the discussion to identify students' knowledge and/or misconceptions about what lies between the earth's surface and the center of the earth.

If students have not read "What Is Under Earth's Surface?" on page 141, they will need to know the information below. The gaps in their prior knowledge should determine what information you share.

- Earth is made of three major layers.
- The outer layer is called the *crust*, which is made up of rock. The crust is covered by soil or water.
- The bottom of the crust is hot enough to melt some of the rock. The melted rock is called *magma*.
- Earth's middle layer is called the *mantle*. The mantle is mostly solid hot rock. This layer is much thicker than the crust and twice as hot.
- The deepest layer is the *core*, made up of two parts—the outer core and the inner core. The outer core is liquid metal and hotter than the mantle. The inner core, which is the center of the earth, is solid even though it is the hottest of Earth's layers.

Preteach Vocabulary

Preteach the following words from "Journey Beneath the Earth" using the Vocabulary Routine on page 29. Or you may wish to use the concept circles shown in the sidebar.

Define each word and provide an example sentence. Also point out multiple meanings and related words.

- **plates:** huge sections of the earth's crust that float on the mantle. *Earth's crust and the upper part of the mantle are divided into plates.* Point out that *plates* is a word that has multiple meanings. Ask students to give examples of some of the other meanings: for example, dishes; in baseball, home plate; a thin sheet of glass; license plate.
- **collide:** crash. *The truck skidded on the ice and collided into a fence.*
- **trench:** a long, narrow opening in the earth; a ditch. *The forest rangers dug a deep trench at the edge of the woods to halt the spread of the fire.*
- **lava:** hot, melted rock that flows from an active volcano. *The lava erupting from the volcano could be seen from miles away.*

Read the Selection

- Distribute copies of "Journey Beneath the Earth," pages 146–147. Have students preview the selection using the Preview Routine on page 41. Then guide students as they apply the strategies they have learned for navigating text and reading a diagram.
- Before the second read, use the Minilesson to teach students about the selection's text structure: cause and effect.

Minilesson

Teaching the Text Structure: Cause and Effect

Introduce: Remind students of the importance of identifying how text is structured—it helps them organize their thinking as they read. Explain that recognizing a cause and effect text structure in a science book will help them understand how processes in science work—what things happen and why they happen.

Model: You may wish to use the Think Aloud to model how to determine the text structure of the section "The Ring of Fire."

Guided Practice/Apply: As students reread the first two paragraphs of the selection, help them complete the graphic organizer for cause and effect, page 145. Then have them fill out, on their own, another cause-and-effect organizer to show what happened when the Nevado del Ruiz volcano erupted.

Point out to students that paying attention to cause and effect helps them understand how a scientific process works.

Think Aloud

On page 147, I learn how volcanoes on the Ring of Fire form. The process begins when the moving plates collide. The collision makes one plate slide under the other. This is an example of cause and effect. The fact that the plates collide is the cause. The effect is that one plate slides under the other. The diagram helps me visualize what happens.

Even though there are no clue words, I see that the organization of the paragraph is cause and effect. So, as I continue reading, I look for the next cause and effect. Next, the sliding plate enters the hot mantle. This causes the rocks in the plate to melt, forming magma. That is the effect. When I finish reading the paragraph, I understand the chain of cause-and-effect events that leads to the formation of volcanoes.

Making a graphic organizer to show each cause and effect will help me remember what happened and why it happened.

Comprehension QuickCheck

After you have completed the lesson, you may use the following questions to check students' comprehension.

1. *What are some of the special features in this text? How do they help you?* (Answers should show an understanding of how maps and diagrams help the reader visualize the text.)

2. *What helped you figure out the text structure of "Ring of Fire"?* (Answers will vary.)

3. *How did knowing the text structure help you?* (It helps you anticipate what you're going to read; you can look for each cause and effect.)

4. *What happens to the sliding plate when it slides under another plate?* (Rocks in the sliding plate melt and form magma which then forms a volcano.)

Possible Answers

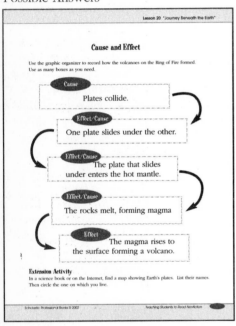

Independent Practice: Writing

Have students write a summary of the information they read in "Journey Beneath the Earth." Suggest that they use the graphic organizers they completed while reading to help them create their summaries. Have them include the following:

• what the Ring of Fire is,

• where it is found,

• how it was formed.

Web Links

kids.earth.nasa.gov

"For Kids Only—Earth Science Enterprise" from NASA

volcano.und.nodak.edu

Volcano World

Cause and Effect

Use the graphic organizer to record how the volcanoes on the Ring of Fire formed. Use as many boxes as you need.

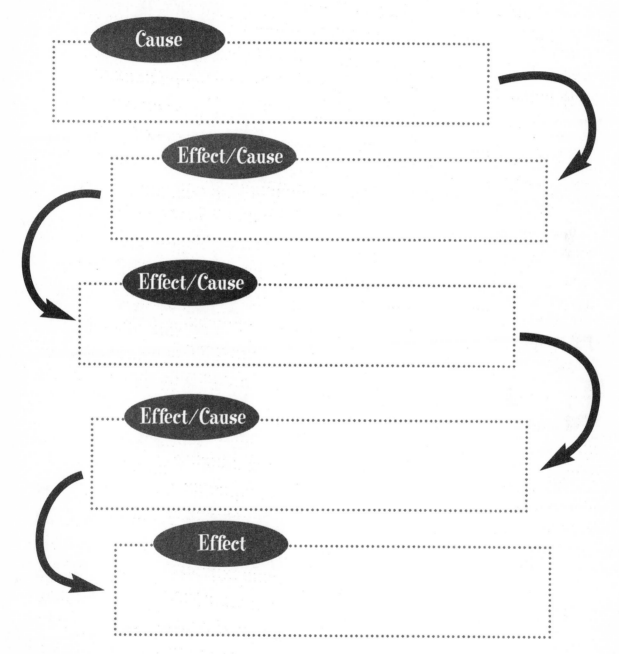

Extension Activity

In a science book or on the Internet, find a map showing Earth's plates. List their names. Then circle the one on which you live.

Journey Beneath the Earth

Plates, Pieces of a Puzzle

Your home is the place where you live. It's also the **plate** on which you live. That's because Earth's crust and the upper part of the mantle are divided into sections. Each section is called a plate. These plates fit together like the pieces of a jigsaw puzzle. But unlike a jigsaw puzzle, the plates are always slowly moving. In some places, the plates are pulling apart. In some places, they are slowly sliding past one another. In other places the plates are colliding, creating trenches or mountain ranges.

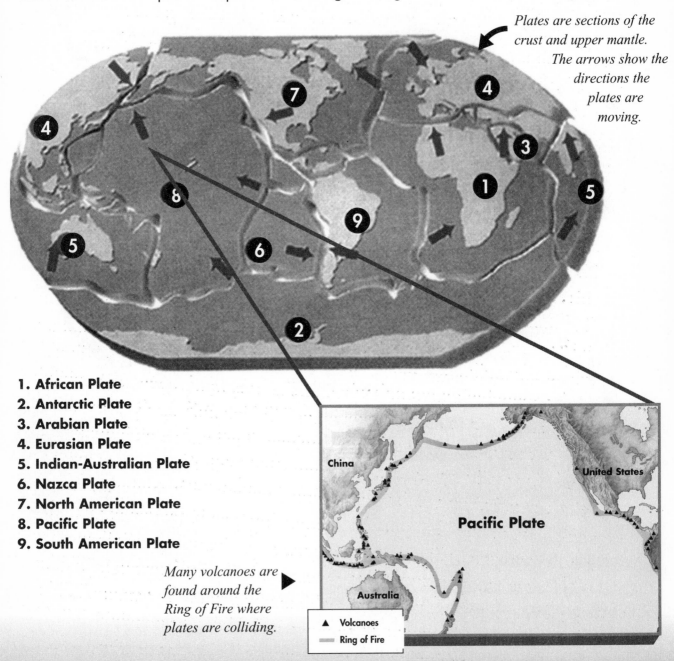

Plates are sections of the crust and upper mantle. The arrows show the directions the plates are moving.

1. **African Plate**
2. **Antarctic Plate**
3. **Arabian Plate**
4. **Eurasian Plate**
5. **Indian-Australian Plate**
6. **Nazca Plate**
7. **North American Plate**
8. **Pacific Plate**
9. **South American Plate**

Many volcanoes are found around the Ring of Fire where plates are colliding.

China

United States

Pacific Plate

Australia

▲ Volcanoes
▬ Ring of Fire

Teaching Students to Read Nonfiction

The Ring of Fire

There are about 500 active volcanoes on Earth—volcanoes that have erupted in the past 50 years. More than 300 of them are found on the Ring of Fire. The Ring of Fire is a giant ring of volcanoes that surrounds the Pacific Plate.

The volcanoes on the Ring of Fire form where the huge moving plates collide. The diagram at the bottom of the page shows what can happen when one of these rocky plates slides under another plate. In the diagram, the front edge of the left plate is sliding under the front edge of the right plate. As the left plate slides down into the earth, it enters the hot mantle. Rocks in the sliding plate begin to melt, and the melting rocks form **magma**. The magma then rises to the surface, and a volcano forms.

The sliding of one plate under another is called subduction. A deep trench usually forms in the area where subduction begins. Sometimes the volcanoes form an evenly spaced line that follows the trench. You can see the line of volcanoes in the picture. In the Ring of Fire, many volcanoes that were formed by subduction appear along the western edge of the American continents. Three of these volcanoes, one in South America, one in Central America, and one in North America, erupted in the 1980s. The eruption of the Nevado del Ruiz volcano in South America melted large amounts of snow. The melted snow created mudflows. The mudflows swept through towns and villages, killed thousands of people, and caused great property damage.

Other subduction volcanoes along the Ring of Fire first erupted under the ocean. Then, as the lava continued to flow, the lava built up in the volcano. Over time, the lava built up enough to rise above the ocean's surface, creating an island. The country of Japan, for example, is made of a gently curving chain of islands that formed from volcanoes. Mount Fuji, in Japan, may be the most famous volcano in the world. Its lovely snow-capped peak has inspired painters, poets, and other people for thousands of years.

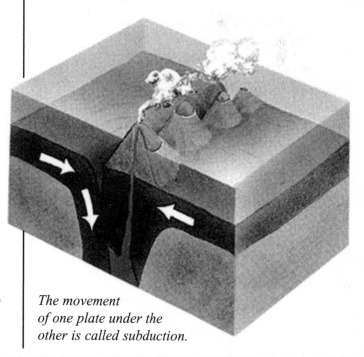

The movement of one plate under the other is called subduction.

From DISCOVER THE WONDER Grade 4. Copyright © 1993, 1994 by Scott, Foresman and Company. Reprinted by permission of Pearson Education Inc.

How to Read a Social Studies Textbook

Multiple Features of Social Studies Textbooks

Reading a social studies textbook is similar to reading a science textbook (see Lesson 19). Students will probably recognize that both kinds of textbooks have many features in common. You may want to acknowledge once again that textbooks can look daunting because

1. their pages often have several different type sizes and type faces;

2. in addition to text, there are often many other elements on a page, such as maps, graphs, and diagrams.

Why Are They Useful?

Remind students that textbooks include many features to make them "student friendly."

- The *chapter title* and the *headings* name the topic and tell the reader what the main ideas are.

- The *boldfaced words* signal important vocabulary.

- The *graphic aids* illustrate information in the text and/or provide additional facts.

The more familiar students become with these features and the more proficient they are in using them, the more accessible textbooks will be.

———————————————— ✳ ————————————————

Direct Instruction

- Distribute the Social Studies lesson, pages 150–151. Have students read it silently before discussing the model text together. Then display the *color transparency* and use it to guide students as they read and use the Reading Tools.

- Use the Minilesson to teach students how to read a historical map.

Materials

✳ Model Text, "The Country Doubles Its Size," p. 151

✳ Text Structure Transparency 15

✳ Bookmark, p. 160

Teaching the Text Feature

Introduce: Explain to students that the map on page 151 is a historical map. A **historical map** provides information about the land area of a particular place sometime in the past. A historical map:

1. illustrates information in the text and enables the reader to visualize it.

2. gives the reader additional information by showing the "big picture."

3. allows the reader to understand the results of an event, such as the Louisiana Purchase.

Model: Use the Think Aloud to model how to read a historical map.

Guided Practice/Apply: Ask students to tell what they learned from the map. Then have them answer the question posed in the caption. You may also wish to ask the following:

1. *What natural feature became the western boundary of the United States in 1803?* (the Continental Divide or the Rocky Mountains)

2. *After the Louisiana Purchase, what countries still claimed land in what is now the United States?* (Spain and Great Britain)

Comprehension QuickCheck

After you have completed the lesson, you may use the following questions to check students' comprehension:

1. *What special features were in the text, and how did you use them?* (Answers should include the use of the selection title and headings, the boldfaced words, and the map.)

2. *What did you learn from the map that you didn't know before?* (Answers will vary.)

3. *What are some of the present-day states located in what was the Louisiana Purchase?* (Answers will include Minnesota, Iowa, Missouri, Arkansas, Louisiana, North and South Dakota, Nebraska, Kansas, Oklahoma, and parts of Montana, Wyoming, and Colorado.)

4. *How do you think our country's history might have been different if Jefferson had not bought the Louisiana Territory?* (Answers will vary.)

5. *The text talks about the "farmers who lived in the West." What was the West before 1803?* (the Indiana Territory, Kentucky, Tennessee, and the Mississippi Territory—the land just east of the Mississippi River)

The first thing I notice is that the map is very different from a map of the United States today. The map shows the United States at the time of the Louisiana Purchase. It helps me understand the importance of that event.

For example, I see that New Orleans is at the mouth of the Mississippi River, on the Gulf of Mexico. The text says that New Orleans was vital to farmers. Now I understand why. The port made it possible for farmers to sell their crops abroad, so it was important for the United States to control it.

I also see how huge an area the Louisiana Purchase was. It was about the same size as what was then the whole United States. The Louisiana Purchase made our country twice as big. That's amazing!

Looking at the map makes me realize that United States history would certainly have been very different if the Louisiana Purchase had not happened.

Social Studies Textbook

Reading a social studies textbook is a lot like reading a science textbook. The subject matter is different, of course. A social studies textbook contains information about people, places, cultures, and historical events. But like a science text, a social studies book has features that are there to guide you as you read.

If you look through a social studies textbook, you'll notice some things that are probably familiar to you—chapter titles, headings, boldfaced words. You'll also see graphic aids, such as maps, charts, and graphs. The graphic aid on page 151 is a historical map. You may not recognize it at first, because it shows the United States of 1803. It is there to help you picture the historical events that are in the text.

Reading Tools

In this lesson, you will be reading about the Louisiana Purchase, from a social studies textbook. Use the tools below to help you as you read.

- Read the **title** and **introduction** to learn what the chapter is about.

- Read the **headings**. They outline the main ideas in the text.

- After your **preview**, jot down what you think the chapter will be about. When you finish reading, go back and see if you were correct.

- As you read, pay special attention to **boldfaced words**. They are important vocabulary terms.

- The writer may ask you to stop reading and look at the **graphic aid** because it illustrates an idea in the text. In this lesson, the graphic aid is a map. When you finish studying it, go back to the place in the text where you left off and continue reading.

- Read the **caption** that goes with the graphic aid. Captions often provide additional information.

- Answer any **questions** in the text to help you check your understanding.

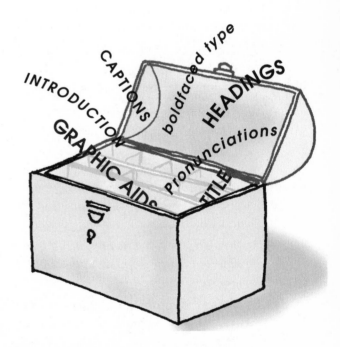

Remember to use these Reading Tools when you read a social studies textbook.

The Country Doubles Its Size

A. The Importance of New Orleans

Up until the mid-1700s, France claimed all the land between the Mississippi River and the Rocky Mountains. France called this area Louisiana. In 1763 France gave Louisiana to Spain. France also gave Spain the most important place in this huge area, the port city of New Orleans, near the mouth of the Mississippi River.

Look at the map below. You can see why the port of New Orleans was vital to farmers who lived in the West. These farmers sent their crops to market down the Mississippi River to New Orleans. At the port in New Orleans the crops were loaded onto oceangoing ships and sent to Europe and the West Indies.

In 1802, Spain announced that western farmers could no longer use New Orleans. Even worse, President Jefferson learned that Spain had secretly given back all of Louisiana, including New Orleans, to France. He knew that the French emperor, Napoleon, wanted to build a new empire in the Americas.

B. The United States Purchases the Louisiana Territory

Jefferson decided to try to buy the port city of New Orleans from the French. He sent two representatives to France to make an offer of $10 million for the port.

At that time France was having a short period of peace in its long war with Great Britain. But the French government knew that war would soon start again. The French needed money for that war. Also, although Jefferson did not know it, Napoleon had given up his ideas about starting a new French empire in North America. Napoleon knew he could not defend Louisiana against the British navy once the war started again.

So when the American representatives offered to pay the French $10 million for New Orleans, they were amazed by France's reply. No, said the French, we are not interested in selling New Orleans by itself. But if you would like to buy all of Louisiana, including New Orleans, for $15 million, perhaps we can make a deal.

The Americans quickly accepted the offer, and in 1803 the United States bought the large piece of land. This land was called the **Louisiana Purchase**. The whole territory cost the United States a few pennies an acre. It was the biggest bargain in American history.

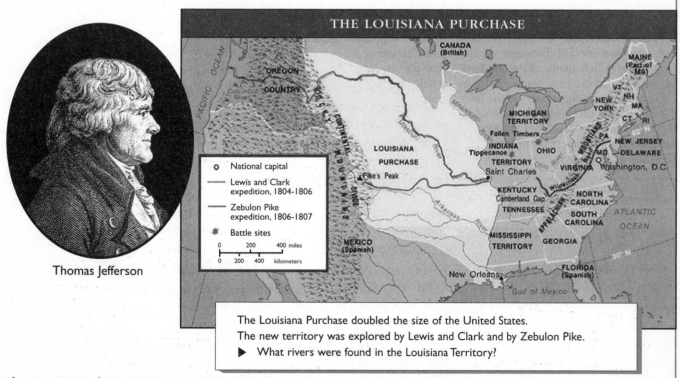

Thomas Jefferson

THE LOUISIANA PURCHASE

○ National capital
— Lewis and Clark expedition, 1804-1806
— Zebulon Pike expedition, 1806-1807
✳ Battle sites

0   200   400 miles
0   200   400   kilometers

The Louisiana Purchase doubled the size of the United States.
The new territory was explored by Lewis and Clark and by Zebulon Pike.
▶ What rivers were found in the Louisiana Territory?

excerpt from page 331-333 of OUR COUNTRY. Copyright (c) 1995 by Silver Burdett Ginn Inc. Reprinted by permission of Pearson Education, Inc

Reading "The Fight for Suffrage"

Build Background

Students will read a section of social studies text that deals with women's suffrage. To appreciate the difficulties that women faced in the fight to obtain suffrage, students will have to understand the laws and prevailing attitudes toward women in the mid-1800s. Create a blank Smart Chart and distribute copies or create one on butcher paper. Use the routine on page 24. Through your questioning, guide the discussion to identify students' knowledge and/or misconceptions about the rights of women in the mid-1800s.

The gaps in students' background knowledge should determine what information you share prior to reading.

- In the middle 1800s, women did not have equal rights with men. When a woman married, everything she owned became the property of her husband.
- Women were not allowed to vote.
- Women were expected to be "seen and not heard."
- Women had little opportunity to attend school beyond the early grades.
- In 1848 Elizabeth Cady Stanton and Lucretia Mott organized a convention on women's rights. It was held in Seneca Falls, New York. Hundreds of women attended the meeting, including Susan B. Anthony.

Preteach Vocabulary

Preteach the words below using the Vocabulary Routine on page 29. Or you may wish to use the Word Connection Chart shown in the sidebar. Define each word and provide an example sentence.

- **suffrage:** The right to vote. *In the 1800's, women could not take part in elections because they did not have suffrage.* A woman who fought for women's right to vote was known as a suffragette.
- **public office:** A position in national, state, or local government. *My neighbor holds public office as a member of the School Board.*

Materials

✳ Model Text, "The Fight for Suffrage," pp. 156–157

✳ Graphic Organizer, p. 155

Word Connection

Write each pair of words on the chalkboard. Have students discuss how the words are related.

public office .... **legislature**

(A legislature is made up of legislators who hold public office.)

bill ...... **legislature**

(A bill is a proposed law. If it is voted on and passed, it may become an amendment to the Constitution.)

suffrage .... **public office**
...... **legislature**

(Citizens who have suffrage elect people to public office, including the legislature.)

- **bill:** (n) A proposed law. *The state Senate voted in favor of a bill to make Morgan Woods a state park.* Point out that *bill* is a word that has multiple meanings: a statement of money owed, e.g., a bill from a store; the beak of a bird; paper money.

- **legislature:** A group of men and women who make the laws of a country or a state. *There is an election for our state legislature in November.* The root *leg* is derived from the Latin *lex*, which means "law." Related words are *legal* and *legislate*.

- **amendment:** A change of a law or the Constitution. *The suffragettes demanded an amendment to the Constitution allowing women to vote.*

Read the Selection

- Distribute copies of "The Fight for Suffrage," pages 156–157. Have students preview the selection. During the reading, guide students as they apply the strategies they have learned. Point out that the selection also contains primary source material.

- Before the second reading, use the Minilesson below to teach students about the selection's text structure: problem and solution.

Minilesson

Teaching the Text Structure: Problem and Solution

Introduce: Point out that *all* the information in a social studies text may not fall neatly into just one text structure. For example, a writer talking about the causes and effects of a long drought may also compare and contrast the situation in different parts of the country. Or if the writer describes the effects of the drought over several years, that information might be organized in a sequence.

Explain that a writer often provides signals, such as special key words, to tell the reader what the main text structure is. Students should look for these signals as they read.

Model: Use the Think Aloud to model how to identify the text structure.

Guided Practice/Apply: As students reread the selection, have them complete the graphic organizer for problem and solution, page 155. Then have them summarize orally the steps taken to solve the problem, using their graphic organizers for reference.

Think Aloud

Writers give us clues as to how they have organized their writing. In the first paragraph of "The Fight for Suffrage," the writer says, "They discussed the problem of how women could win a wide variety of rights…" This is a signal that the writer is going to identify a problem, that women couldn't vote, and then explain the steps that were taken to solve the problem.

This is what happens in the rest of the chapter. I also see that the writer presents the solutions in chronological order. That makes sense. If the writer had jumped back and forth in time, it would have been very confusing. By the end of the chapter, I learned how the problem of women's suffrage was solved over the years.

Comprehension QuickCheck

After the lesson, you may wish to ask the following:

1. *How did knowing the text structure help you?* (Answers should include that knowing the text structure helped them identify the problem and look for solutions as they read.)

2. *What information did you learn from the primary sources in the text?* (Stanton's letter showed how hard she and Anthony worked for the suffrage movement; it also revealed that, by traveling and speaking extensively, she did not conform to the expectations for women at the time. The photos showed that the suffrage movement included women of all ages, the clothing of the different time periods, and the way people voted in 1920. The quotes expressed the pride Morris and Ross felt about their roles.)

3. *Which of the primary sources provide facts? Which express opinions?* (Stanton's letter and the photos provide factual information. The quotes from Morris and Ross express opinions.)

4. *Compare the number of women in Congress in 1950 and 2001.* (about seven times more women in Congress in 2001.)

Independent Practice: Writing

Have students write a summary of the information they read in "The Fight for Suffrage." Suggest that they use the problem and solution graphic organizer they completed while reading to help them.

Possible Answers

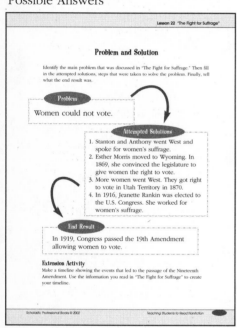

```
┌──────────────────────────────────────────────────────────┐
:                                                            :
:                     Web Links                              :
:                                                            :
:   www.nwhp.org              National Women's History Project
:   www.greatwomen.org        National Women's Hall of Fame  :
:   bensguide.gpo.gov         Ben's Guide to American        :
:                               Government                   :
:                                                            :
:   gi.grolier.com/presidents/nbk/   Grolier (president biographies)
:     prescont.html                                          :
:   www.americanpresidents.org/   U.S. President Biographies :
:                                                            :
└──────────────────────────────────────────────────────────┘
```

Problem and Solution

Identify the main problem that was discussed in "The Fight for Suffrage." Then fill in the attempted solutions—steps that were taken to solve the problem. Finally, tell what the end result was.

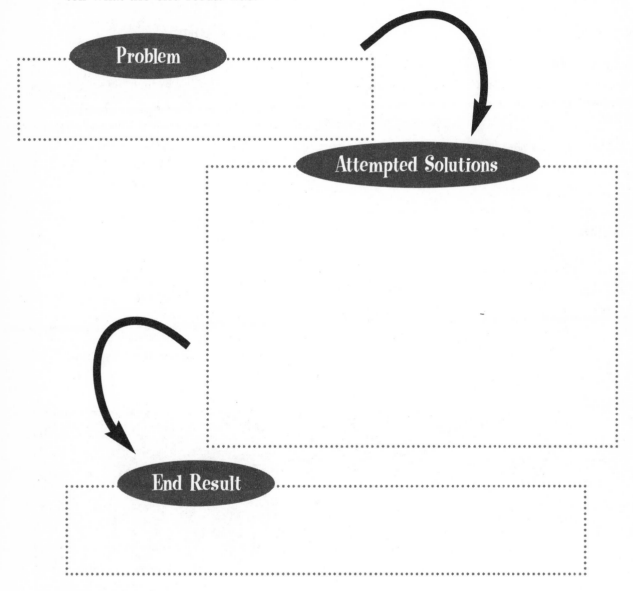

Extension Activity

Make a time line showing the events that led to the passage of the Nineteenth Amendment. Use the information you read in "The Fight for Suffrage" to create your time line.

The Fight for Suffrage

In 1851 Susan B. Anthony met Elizabeth Cady Stanton at Seneca Falls, New York. They discussed the problem of how women could win a wide variety of rights, such as voting, holding public office, and service on juries. For the next 50 years, they led the fight for women's suffrage.

Suffrage in the West

During the 1860s and 1870s Stanton and Anthony traveled to the West. In an 1871 letter Stanton described a trip to Utah:

> Susan and I are slowly journeying Westward.
> Since I left you, I have filled twenty engagements
> [appointments], speaking twice in nearly
> every place.

Gradually the suffrage movement gained support in the West. The women who lived in the West had made a difficult journey. In small communities they worked alongside men in jobs women did not usually have. They were ready to take a role in citizenship. Many men there agreed. These men had started new lives and were open to new ideas. Women's suffrage was one of them.

A First for Women

In 1869 only about 1,000 women lived in all of Wyoming. One of those women, Esther Morris of South Pass City, had just arrived from Illinois.

Morris was a strong speaker who supported women's suffrage. She helped convince the lawmakers to create a bill giving women the right to vote. In December 1869 the legislature passed a law declaring that "every woman of the age of twenty-one years residing in this territory may at every election… cast her vote."

Some of the lawmakers who voted for the bill thought that it would encourage women to live in Wyoming. A delighted Susan B. Anthony urged her followers to move there. One year later the women of the Utah Territory won the same right.

Another victory happened in Wyoming. In 1870

Women all across the United States held parades for suffrage.

Library of Congress

Scholastic Professional Books © 2002   *Teaching Students to Read Nonfiction*

the government appointed the first woman ever to serve as a judge. The judge was Esther Morris. She said her position was "a test of a woman's ability to hold public office." She inspired women all over the United States.

An Amendment

In Wyoming women could vote, but not in many other states. In some states women could vote for President, but not in other elections.

To grant women throughout our country the right to vote, Congress would have to pass an amendment to the Constitution. But who would fight for such an amendment in Congress?

The answer came in 1916. In that year Montana voters elected Jeannette Rankin to the House of Representatives. She was the first woman ever to serve in Congress.

Rankin worked hard for the women's suffrage amendment. She made speeches and tried to convince other representatives to support it.

As a result, in 1919 Congress passed the Nineteenth Amendment to the Constitution. The state legislatures approved it the next year. Women's right to vote became our law at last.

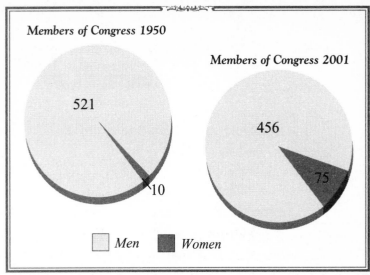

Members of Congress 1950

521

10

Members of Congress 2001

456

75

☐ Men   ■ Women

Wyoming's Governor

The struggle for equal rights did not end with the Nineteenth Amendment. Women continued to work for equality. Some years later another victory for women took place in Wyoming. In 1924 Wyoming voters elected Nellie Tayloe Ross as their governor. She was the first woman to serve as a governor in our country's history. More than 50 years later, on her 100th birthday, Ross was quoted as saying that her career marked "a milestone in the battle for women's equality."

(above) Elizabeth Cady Stanton and Susan B. Anthony.
© Bettmann/CORBIS

(left) Women vote for the first time after the Nineteenth Amendment is passed by Congress in 1919.
© Bettmann/CORBIS

from *Regions: Adventure in Time and Place.* Copyright © 1997 Macmillan/McGraw-Hill., a Division of the Educational and Professional Publishing Group of the McGraw-Hill Companies.

Bibliography

Alvermann, Donna E. and Stephen F. Phelps. 1998. *Content Reading and Literacy: Succeeding in Today's Diverse Classrooms.* Second Edition. Needham Heights, Massachusetts: Allyn & Bacon.

Carnine, Douglas W., Jerry Silbert, Edward J. Kameenui. 1997. *Direct Instruction Reading.* Third Edition. Upper Saddle River, New Jersey: Prentice-Hall.

Cooper, J. David. 1993. Literacy: *Helping Children Construct Meaning.* Second Edition. Boston: Houghton Mifflin Company.

CORE (Consortium on Reading Excellence). 1999. Arena Press, Novato, CA.

Lapp, Diane, James Flood, and Nancy Farnan. 1996. *Content Area Reading and Learning: Instructional Strategies.* Second Edition. Needham Heights, Massachusetts: Allyn & Bacon.

Vacca, Richard T. and Jo Anne L. Vacca. 1999. *Content Area Reading: Literacy and Learning Across the Curriculum.* Sixth Edition. New York, N.Y.: Addison-Wesley Educational Publishers Inc.

Web Links

www.scholastic.com	Scholastic
teacher.scholastic.com/newszone/index.asp	Scholastic (current events)
www.grolier.com	Grolier (nonfiction books)
www.sln.org	The Science Learning Network
www.historyplace.com/index.html	The History Place
www.s9.com/biography	Biographical Dictionary
www.graphic.org	Graphic Organizers
www.educationplanet.com	Education Planet
www.homeworkcentral.com	Homework Central
www.mcn.edu/sitesonline.htm	The Museum Guide
www.edhelper.com	EdHelper.com (lesson plans)
www.ed.gov/free	FREE (Federal Resources for Educational Excellence)
www.pbs.org/teachersource	PBS
school.discovery.com/schoolhome.html	Discovery Channel School
www.odci.gov/cia/publications/factbook	The World Book Factbook
www.mcrel.org/whelmers	McRel Science Activities

Related Internet Reference Books

Homework on the Internet by Marianne J. Dyson (Scholastic, 2000)

1001 Best Websites for Educators by Timothy Hopkins (Teacher Created Materials, 2001)

Internet Made Easy: 10 Quick & Fun Internet Field Trips by Deirdre Kelly (Scholastic, 2000)

Bookmarks

Lesson 1

How to Read Nonfiction Text

- ✔ *Preview* the article.
- ✔ Read the *title, introduction,* and *headings* to learn the main ideas.
- ✔ *Predict* what the article will be about.
- ✔ Notice the *special features* that are included.
- ✔ As you read, pay special attention to the *bold-faced words*.
- ✔ Use the *pronunciations*.
- ✔ Study the *graphic aids* and read the *captions* carefully.

Lesson 2

How to Read a Magazine Article

- ✔ *Preview* the article.
- ✔ Read the *title, deck,* and *headings* to learn the main ideas.
- ✔ *Predict* what the article will be about.
- ✔ Notice the *special features* that are included.
- ✔ As you read, pay special attention to the *bold-faced words*.
- ✔ Use the *pronunciations*.
- ✔ Study the *graphic aids* and read the *captions* carefully.

Lesson 3

How to Read a Map

- ✔ Read the map *title*.
- ✔ Find the *symbols*.
- ✔ Look at the map *key*.
- ✔ Read the *labels* on the map.
- ✔ Find the map *scale*.
- ✔ Find the *compass rose*.

Lesson 5

How to Read a Circle Graph

- ✔ Read the *title* of the graph. Think about what the topic is.
- ✔ Look at each *part* of the graph and read each *label*.
- ✔ Think about what information is represented.

How to Read a Line Graph

- ✔ Read the *title* to find out the topic of the graph.
- ✔ Look at each *label*. Think about what the numbers stand for.
- ✔ To read the graph, use your finger to trace from each dot to the side and the bottom.
- ✔ Think about the *comparisons* the graph is making.

Lesson 7

How to Read Primary Sources

- ✔ First, read the *title*.
- ✔ *Preview* the text to learn about the topic.
- ✔ Read the *main article*.
- ✔ Read the *primary source* material. Ask yourself, "How does this information add to what I know about the topic?"

Lesson 9

How to Read Reference Sources

- ✔ Look up your topic in the *table of contents* or *index*.
- ✔ *Preview* the text.
- ✔ Use the *special features* as you read.
- ✔ Think about what information the *primary sources* add.

Lesson 11

How to Read an Online Encyclopedia Article

✔ First, read the *title* to learn what the article is about.

✔ Scan for *subheadings* to identify the main ideas in the text.

✔ Click on the *site search button* to be taken to other parts of the Web site.

✔ Look for other text features such as *photographs*, *links*, *maps*, *special boxes*, and *underlined topics*.

Lesson 13

How to Read Online News Articles

✔ Read the *title*.

✔ Look for a *date*.

✔ Click on the *illustration* to make it larger and then read the caption.

✔ Click on the *underlined words* in the article for more information.

✔ Look for *buttons*.

Lesson 15

How to Read Periodicals

✔ First, look in the *table of contents*.

✔ *Preview* the text as you would do with any non-fiction.

✔ Then *read the text* to learn about your topic.

✔ If the text includes *photographs or charts*, study them carefully.

Lesson 17

How to Read Multi-Tiered Time Lines

✔ First, read the *title*.

✔ Look at the titles of each *tier*.

✔ Find the starting and ending *dates*.

✔ Read the *labels* for each date.

Lesson 19

How to Read a Science Textbook

✔ Read the lesson *title* and *introduction* to learn the topic of the lesson.

✔ Read the *headings* to find out the main ideas.

✔ Remember the *boldfaced words*.

✔ Study the *graphic aids*.

✔ Answer to yourself the *questions* in the text.

Lesson 21

How to Read a Social Studies Textbook

✔ Read the lesson *title*, *introduction*, and *headings*.

✔ Decide what the *topic* and *main ideas* of the lesson are.

✔ Remember the *boldfaced words*.

✔ Study the *graphic aid* and read the *caption*.

✔ Answer any *questions* in the text.